Reactions to

This fast-moving, exciting and insightf
think about who you are and where yo
—Brian Tracy, Author, *The Way to Wealth*

Release has changed my life in profound ways. I have found no
other book that is so simple to read, yet has such a unique ability
to initiate deep self-reflection in the reader. This self-reflection is
bound to put your life on a new, exciting course. I have bought
several copies and am giving them out as gifts to all my close
friends and family members for Christmas this year!
—Sarah Taylor, MBA
CEO, Taylor Presentations Inc.

Your new book Release is amazing. I had a hard time putting it
down because I couldn't wait to see what was going to unfold on
each and every page... Your skill in weaving essential messages into
a story is terrific... I will be reading it again as I work to implement
the core concepts you conveyed.
So many people need this book. It gives a message of understanding,
clarity and hope. The story is so powerful that I encourage you to
put together some workshops or coaching programs for the many
people who need to learn from your wisdom.
—Wayne Cotton
CEO, Cotton Systems

Not only has it had a significant effect on my own life and outlook,
I have had the opportunity to give copies to friends, colleagues and
family who could use a nudge to move their life forward.
—Linda Edgecombe
Award Winning Speaker, Best Selling Author,
Accountability Expert

It reads like a hot knife through butter, as it cuts to the heart, spreads
the emotions, sharpens the mind and releases the soul.
—Sandra Logan
Unbiased friend of the author

Release

A Wilderness Adventure of the Soul

DAREN WRIDE

Deep Wild Communications

Library and Archives Canada Cataloguing in Publication

Wride, Daren , 1964-
    Release: A Wilderness Adventure of the Soul / Daren Wride

ISBN 978-09783393-0-2

    1. Self-actualization (Psychology) I. Title

BF637.S4W74 2008   158.1   C2007-903593-0

Sketches: Dave Watland
Cover Design: Cathi Stevenson

Printed in Canada

For My Creator, the Giver of Release

Author's Note to the Reader

Each of us is on a journey. But it's tragically easy to walk the beaten path over and over again — never learning, never growing, never gaining ground. We become masters of our work, sculptors of our bodies, and experts in shallow relationships, while too often failing to cultivate our souls and reach the destinations we truly crave. In moments of vulnerability, we might admit that we can't even identify those desired destinations. Why? Because this all takes time — unrushed time, reflection, solitude. And in much of the world today there is no rarer commodity.

The thought of going on a wilderness trek, like the one undertaken by the character in this story, may be exciting to you and something you will begin to plan even as you read. Or it may be an overwhelming idea, a true impossibility at this stage of your life. In either case, you are fully capable of taking the more significant inner journey, and making many of the same discoveries our traveler makes along the way. But to do this, you must add to your reading those rare ingredients of unrushed time, reflection, and solitude. Read slowly. Journal your thoughts. Allow the principles to soak into both your head and your heart.

A mentor once instructed, "If it doesn't work at home, don't export it!" I have followed that advice in the writing of this book. As a result, what you will find in these pages is not merely a theory of personal discovery and growth, or some random thoughts strung together in an afternoon. This is the systemization of a process I've lived through, which was forged in my real world of crisis, pain, success, and joy. As I shared different aspects of this process informally, and in talks given in a variety of settings, I was surprised by the response. The principles

I shared struck an immediate chord and helped many people progress on their journeys in very specific ways. I quickly realized that these principles I've discovered through my reading, writing, reflecting, counseling, and teaching, and then applied to my own life, had a universal quality which would benefit many. This book is the result of that discovery, and an attempt to make these principles and the *Release* process accessible to more people than I could ever meet with personally.

My prayer for you, and for every person who launches out on the Adventure of the Soul, is this: May you be released to more clearly see both your place in this world and the Creator's heart for you. And may you have the courage to take the next step on your journey, wherever it leads.

Press on!

Daren Wride
Lake Country, British Columbia

Day 1

The last ribbon of light along the horizon was fading, and the August air was cool. The base camp was situated halfway up a mountain in a stand of parkland pine. All the buildings were log, except for a tin generator shed set well back of the main lodge. I was greeted by a large, friendly dog. As I got out of my rented pick-up, the lodge door opened, and Len, director of the base, walked across the deck and down the stairs to greet me.

"Welcome to *Release*!" he said with a smile, hand extended. "We can unload your gear later. You've just got time to grab a bite and get to the general orientation."

Twenty minutes later I found myself seated in a rustic conference room with two other guests and the entire staff of five.

"Again, let me welcome each of you to the *Release* adventure," Len began. "You are on the cusp of what may be the most significant personal growth journey of your lives."

I knew his claim wasn't overstated. I'd checked with a half dozen former participants randomly selected from the alumni listing. Each one — without giving away specific details of the program — strongly encouraged me to apply, and, if accepted, do whatever I needed to do to go on the trek. One even suggested I quit my job if the boss didn't give me time off. So I applied. Once accepted, I began preparing for this "odyssey," "ordeal," "gut transplant," and "total personality rebirth," as various alumni had described it. I was nervous, hopeful, and curious about what the next several days would bring. I knew I needed change in my life, but I couldn't define exactly what that change was or how to make it happen.

"This is Marsha, our survival specialist," Len said as he gestured to a thin but strong-looking woman standing to his far right. "Next to her is Jonathon, our fitness tester. You'll be getting to know him much better early tomorrow morning," he said with a grin, causing me and the other guests to glance at each other nervously. "Then we have Randy, our handyman, go-fer, and first-aid officer. He has advanced paramedic training and worked both ambulances and search and rescue for about fifteen years prior to joining us.

"This is my wife, Andrea," he said, gesturing to a smiling fifty-ish woman on his left. "She does our books and is going to serve you your last three decent meals before you head out on your own. She'll have a feast ready for you if and when you arrive back at camp." He said "if" without any hint of humor, and I remembered the three-page notarized waiver I'd read and signed as part of my application process.

Then he launched into a talk he'd obviously given before, but still delivered with genuine passion. "A neutron is released from a uranium atom, traveling at roughly ten million meters per second. This neutron strikes another uranium atom, smashing it into several fragments including two or three more neutrons, which, in turn, smash into a rapidly increasing number of uranium atoms. In very simple terms, this initiates a chain reaction, which, if controlled, becomes nuclear energy, and, if uncontrolled, is a nuclear explosion. In either case, the release of energy is mind-boggling."

"This evening I want you to understand that the picture of a lump of uranium with its unfathomable energy, is a picture of you." He paused for effect, locking eyes solidly with me and the other two guests. "And this is not a flattering, exaggerated picture meant to falsely boost your self esteem. We don't do that here. And we don't have to, because the picture is a true picture, an accurate metaphor for the power, energy, creativity, and potential contained, though perhaps buried, deep inside each one of you."

Len spoke well. He was fluid and energetic without being too flamboyant for such a small group. "The obvious question: How is this personal energy released? In the physical world, scientists have discovered the secret of releasing the power of the atom. They know that if certain steps are followed, the energy will be released. Every time. They gather the right material, in the right quantity, bring it together in the right way, the reaction starts, and the energy is released."

"The same thing can happen for each of you, inside each of you. You must first gather together the right material, the sum total of everything you are today — your experiences, good and bad, and your inherent talents and trained abilities. We refer to this as *Harnessing Your History*. Once you've gathered the raw material, you begin the chain reaction and fire the initial neutron by *Focusing Your Future*. This brings a release of energy and creativity so intense it will surprise, maybe even scare you. Then you will finally be able to do and be what you were created for. We call this *Mastering Your Moment*."

I jotted down the three main points: Harnessing Your History, Focusing Your Future, Mastering Your Moment. It was already more information than I'd gleaned from the website or the alumni I'd contacted. My curiosity about how they were going to deliver on this promise continued to grow.

Len wrapped up his talk by saying, "Do you want it? Do you have the courage to face up to your amazing potential?" He paused to let us think about it. "Most people don't. They don't want the responsibility. They take comfort in their mediocrity, in their self-centered, go-with-the-flow lives. The fact that you're here proves you are not 'most people'. If you push through the challenges of these next several days you will be transformed, and your lives will become part of a powerful chain reaction that is sweeping the planet."

Len stepped back and we applauded. Andrea announced, "There are snacks in the dining room. Feel free to visit for a while, but don't stay up too late! Jonathon will be calling on you at five." My fellow guests and I groaned, but with smiles. We were filled with anticipation for the journey ahead.

We mingled in the dining room for thirty or forty minutes. I chatted briefly with each of the staff and my fellow adventurers. Jennifer was a franchise owner, never married, who I guessed was 38, give or take. Shane was a sales manager with a large corporation. He was married with two kids and had just turned

44 a week earlier. I was the youngest at 35. The minimum age for the course was 25, with no upper age limit, though there were physical fitness standards that had to be met. That was the purpose of the fitness test in the morning. I'd been training four times a week since my acceptance into the program and was confident I'd easily meet the standards.

After the reception I retrieved my gear and found my room. The base grew quiet. I lay awake for a long time reviewing my rationale for coming and wondering what lay ahead. "Why *am* I here?" I asked myself out loud. By most standards I was quite successful. In my late twenties I sold a bicycle shop I'd started in high school and kept through my university years. On the advice of an uncle, I invested much of the modest profit in some junior mining stocks. Base metal prices took off, and when I sold out four years later, again on his advice, I pocketed a mid six-figure profit. The job I held at a marketing firm gave me a comfortable salary. I lived in a condo with no mortgage, traveled four to six weeks each year, and watched my nest egg grow. Though I'd never been married, my girlfriend of three years had been hinting, and I was actively looking for a stone on the sly.

So, the material indications of success were all there. But internally, "spiritually" as a close friend would say, I sensed both fragmentation and a confusing emptiness. I had no purpose in life greater than my own affairs. I often found myself bored, and despite being a lot of fun at a party, I didn't consider myself truly happy. Global issues like poverty, war, and famine bothered me, but I felt helpless to do anything about them, except give a few bucks to charities that seemed to be trying.

I hoped this journey would clarify for me who I was and what I ought to do with the rest of my life. I hoped it would unpack some things I sensed were deep inside, but couldn't yet define or locate. I hoped it would give me a greater sense of purpose. I hoped I would gain a clearer sense of my place in the world. I hoped...

Then I slept.

Day 2

I woke to the sound of gentle thumping on my door, a pause, then thumping on another door, and then a third. A few moments later a voice at my door asked quietly, "Are you awake?"

"Yes," I replied, with nervous anticipation.

"Meet on the deck in ten minutes, dressed for a workout." The voice, which I assumed was Jonathon's, moved to the other guests' rooms as I scrambled out of bed and got ready.

Jennifer and Shane were there when I arrived, bouncing lightly to keep warm. It wasn't below freezing, but we could see our breath. After brief "good mornings" we waited for Jonathon, who showed up looking far too alert and happy. In his colorful workout suit he appeared much more like a trainer than he had the night before. He was toned, but not beefy — lean and proportioned like a decathlete.

"We'll begin with the two-mile run," he explained. "The target is sixteen minutes. I'll run it in fifteen, so you have one minute to finish after me." I wasn't concerned. I'd run six-and-a-half minute miles over five miles in college, and even though I now ran sevens over the same distance, I knew I could do two miles in twelve or thirteen minutes if necessary.

We set off down a trail in the dim but growing light. I stuck to Jonathon's tail; the other two stayed within fifty yards until the end, when I decided to sprint to the finish. Jonathon matched me stride for stride, with ease.

"Good run," he said, already recovering as Jennifer and Shane pulled up about twenty seconds later. "Let's hit the gym."

We were each weighed and given charts showing how much of our respective body mass we were to push, pull, lift, and move at different stations. Tests for flexibility and balance followed. None of us had any trouble. I suspected that like me, the others had been training regularly since acceptance into the program to meet the required standards. After a brief warm down, we were sent to the showers and told breakfast would be served at 7:00 am.

Len's description the night before was accurate. Breakfast was a "decent meal" consisting of waffles, maple syrup, roast potatoes, tiny venison steakettes, and assorted fruits. There were also several drink options. During breakfast, Len outlined the agenda for the day: GPS training in the morning, survival training in the afternoon, and a brief gathering for final instructions in the evening.

*****

18

The GPS training was new to me. I'd heard about the satellite-based "global positioning system" in various news reports, mostly military. I'd also heard of the sport of geocaching, in which participants looked for hidden caches all over the world. But I'd never held a GPS receiver.

Len, who was instructing the segment, explained, "This instrument is a key to your journey. It's how you'll find the checkpoints, the cabins, and, ultimately, the base camp. You must master a few basic procedures before we can safely send you out on your own."

He had us turn on our receivers and set them to "simulation mode," since we were indoors and would not get satellite reception. My screen came to life with seven segments showing different graphics and numbers that made no sense to me at first. Len explained that simulation mode made the receiver appear just as it would if we had full reception outdoors at the camp.

Len walked us through the screen. Elevation, 4470 feet. I was surprised how high the camp was, but realized it explained the cool morning temperature. Accuracy, 30 feet. Len told us the accuracy varied depending on satellite reception. The next line indicated we were in "simulation" mode. A box showed two concentric circles marked N, S, E, W — the four directions. There were several small numbers on the circles indicating the sky location of the satellites the receiver had locked onto. Another box showed the relative strength of the signal from each satellite. At the bottom was a line showing the date and time, and finally two lines in bold, showing our location in latitude and longitude.

Len directed us to push the "page" button. Immediately my screen changed to a small map with a triangle in the center, which Len explained showed our current location. If you walked while in full GPS mode, the point of the triangle showed your direction of travel. There were a few labeled "waypoints" as Len called them, including the base camp. There was also a dotted line on the map that Len said was the road up from the valley. He showed us how to zoom in so that the screen represented only an acre or two, and zoom out so it showed hundreds of square miles.

We went outside for some drills, during which we went off the simulation mode and accessed the satellites. We worked our way individually through an exercise that consisted of going to waypoints around the base and getting new coordinates for the next waypoint, until we arrived back at the start.

"Essentially, that's how you'll be navigating, but on a much larger scale. Since the GPS uses batteries heavily when it's on and you're moving, you should leave it off and only turn it on to check your location and direction of travel from time to time. Almost all your hiking will be on trails of some kind, so there's really no need to leave the receiver on. The batteries in your GPS are fresh. Your kit will contain spares, but if you use the receiver properly you won't need them. The machines are waterproof and shock-proof to a point, so it's unlikely you'll break them."

He showed us how to change the batteries, and then we went to the conference room one by one for a brief examination that put us through the paces of using the GPS. Confident that we knew what we were doing, Len concluded the session and announced that lunch was in half an hour. The morning had flown by. I was hungry despite the fact that I'd eaten a bit too much breakfast.

Lunch was another "decent meal" of do-it-yourself sandwiches and some amazing homemade vegetable soup.

"I really feel like I could find my way around the wilderness!" gushed Jennifer.

"Yeah, I'm with you on that," I said. "But I'm hoping to learn how to find my way around life."

"That'll come," said Len. "Don't you worry."

"Or my money back, right?"

"If you survive," said Len with a wink.

*****

After lunch it was back to the conference room for survival training. Marsha had a table set up with all sorts of paraphernalia, most of which were foreign to me.

"We're going to begin with wild animal awareness," she began. "At this time of year there are really only two creatures to be concerned with: cougars and bears. Deer, elk, and the few moose we have here calved months ago, and their young are already highly mobile. The mothers don't need to defend their young from you — they'll just get up and leave if you get too close. Mother bears, on the other hand, actively protect their young for up to two years. Bears can also be aggressive if you surprise them, or if they feel you're a threat to their food supply. In rare cases, bears have been known to stalk and attack people in a predatory manner."

Shane's hand shot up. "What do you mean 'predatory manner?'" he asked.

"For the purpose of eating you," Marsha replied. "But again, that's rare. There's a good natural food supply in the area. Our greatest concern is that you'll surprise a mother bear and her cubs. This training video will give you the basics."

The lights dimmed and we viewed a forty-five minute presentation designed to prepare forestry workers for bear encounters. It talked about bear identification and habitat, and the use of bear spray. There was some amazing footage of close encounters between people and bears. When it was over I wasn't sure if I was more or less concerned about meeting a bear, but I agreed with the others that we were certainly more equipped to face a bear should it happen. We were then presented with our own canisters of bear spray.

"Always keep it on your belt," Marsha instructed. "There's no point packing it around if you can't get to it when you need it. To my knowledge, no one with bear spray in hand has ever been killed by a bear."

"But they've been chewed up pretty good, eh?" I joked.

"Yeah, probably," Marsha continued, brushing me off. "Now, let's talk about cougars."

A large picture of a lean, hungry-looking mountain lion came onto the screen. "Cougars primarily eat deer, though they are opportunistic and will eat a wide variety of animals. They prefer to stalk their prey and attack from behind, which means that bear spray is pretty much useless against them. Your packs with the bedrolls at the top make it impossible for them to grab you on the neck from behind, but a cat that's having a hard time due to age or injury might take a run at you anyway. In that case, your best defense is a belt knife like this one, which is in your kits. When the cat jumps on you it will try to grab you on the head or neck and hold on. If that happens, unsheathe your knife and stab at any part of it you can reach. People have survived cougar attacks that way. But please understand, it's very unlikely you will even see a cougar, and even less likely you'll be attacked. We simply want you to be prepared, just in case."

"Have there been any cougar or bear attacks in this area?" Jennifer asked.

"Yes, but not in several years. A cross-country skier was seriously injured by a cougar about four years ago, and two hunters were attacked by an old, toothless grizzly the following year as they cleaned an elk. One of them received a concussion and some broken ribs, but they managed to shoot it." Marsha saw us glance at each other and quickly continued, "I've spent the equivalent of several years of my life in the forest around here and have never had a hostile encounter with any animal. It's extremely unlikely that you will. So let's talk about the two biggest dangers you will face: injury and exposure."

"You'll be alone in the wilderness, walking on game trails, crossing streams, climbing over fallen trees, and traversing steep slopes. You'll likely have some minor stumbles and falls, and it's possible you'll have a serious fall. If that happens, we want you to know what to do."

"Each of you will have a two-way radio that's set on the same channel as our base station. When you're on the trail, the base station is monitored around the clock. Every evening when you get to your camp, you'll radio in your location. All of our camps are located in such a way that we have radio communication. If you don't radio in, we'll send out a search party the next morning."

"The next morning!" Jennifer exclaimed. "What if we're injured and lying out in the open somewhere?"

"Bear bait," I said. Shane laughed, and Jennifer punched me on the shoulder.

"That's why you must pay careful attention for the next several minutes. While our camps have radio communication, you'll often be in places where your two-way will not connect with the base. If you fall or slide down a steep slope, there's a very good chance you'll be out of contact. We don't search at night," Marsha said firmly. "It's too dangerous for the searchers. Once the sun goes down you're on your own."

She opened a small pouch containing what looked like a thin piece of tinfoil several feet square. "This is a survival blanket," she said. "It will keep you from hypothermia at this time of year, even if you can't start a fire. You'll each have one in your pack. Each pack will also have waterproof matches," she held up a small canister, "a small hatchet, and a ball of fire starter that can help you get a fire going, even if it's damp. Let's head outside."

We walked over to the fire pit area, which was about twenty feet in diameter, with log benches around the outside, and sand spread around a sunken fire area. Off to one side was a downed tree. Marsha explained how trees were knocked over by wind all the time, and that if we needed to start a fire, the easiest thing to do was find such a tree. "Of course, if you have a broken leg or are otherwise immobilized, you'll have to make due with what you can reach. But this exercise will help. I want each of you, in different spots on the sand, to start a small fire. Your goal is to get pieces at least one inch in diameter burning freely. Go to it!" she said and stepped back to watch.

I wasn't too concerned about the assignment. I'd camped with my family when I was younger, and by trial and error had figured out how to start a fire. I'd even started a brush fire by my elementary school with some friends one noon hour. Not only did it bring the excitement of fire trucks, but two of us were given the rest of the day off.

I gathered a fistful of dry twigs from the bottom of the tree. On top of those I placed some slightly thicker ones. Then I chopped off some larger branches and broke them into foot-long pieces. I used a couple of these to stabilize my first pile of twigs, and then carefully laid a few more on top. One match got the finer twigs burning, and within four minutes I had a nice blaze. Jennifer was also successful in short order, but Shane was getting frustrated.

Marsha walked over and saw that he was trying to get half-inch and larger pieces started with the matches. "A basic guideline is to make sure you have a least a fistful of dry twigs as thin as your match to light first. The next ones can be two or three times that size, and then you can put on one-inch branches. After you have those burning, you could start full-sized logs if you wanted to."

Shane went and got some small twigs, and in another few minutes had a healthy fire going. "Way to go city boy!" Jennifer joked.

"Good job, Shane," Marsha said. "Let's go back inside and finish up."

After a bit more on fire starting and fire safety she retrieved Randy, who did a brief class on self-administered first aid. When he was done, Marsha gave us little coil-bound survival manuals she said we could read if we were laying on our backs somewhere at the bottom of a cliff.

"I think you're as ready as I can get you in the time we have. Supper is in just under an hour. Take a break and we'll see you then."

I put up my hand. "All things considered, is this trip we're heading out on actually dangerous?"

Marsha didn't even pause before answering. "Absolutely. This adventure is about life, and life is dangerous."

I quickly followed up, "Has anyone ever been injured or killed on a *Release* trip?"

"Yes," Marsha replied more softly, but without hesitation. "One lady broke her pelvis in a serious fall. She was rescued. But a 46-year-old man, who looked very healthy on the outside, died of a heart attack on a strenuous section of his course. Injury and death are real possibilities. But think of it this way: It's better to die on a quest to reach your full potential than to never start the journey." We looked at each other for a few seconds while her words hung in the air. "See you at dinner," she said.

*****

Dinner was a feast, capped off by some amazing carrot cake for dessert. As we wound down, Len asked us to meet in the conference room in thirty minutes.

When we gathered, Len walked to the front of the room.

"Well, what's going on for you up here?" he asked, pointing to his head. "Give it to me in one word," he said, pointing at me.

"Anticipation," I answered.

"Curiosity," Shane offered when Len pointed at him.

"Nervous excitement," Jennifer said.

"Ah yes, there's always a person who can't keep it to one word!" Len said. We all laughed.

"Do you have any questions that haven't been answered yet? Is there any way in which you feel unprepared?"

"How long exactly is this journey we're going on?" asked Shane. "We were told to allow three weeks, but no one has said how long we'll be out on our own."

"Usually that question comes much sooner than this!" said Len. "From the time you arrived to the time you leave for home will be three weeks or less."

Shane looked at me and Jennifer in amazement, then back at Len. "Can't you tell us any more than that?"

"No, that would spoil it. You don't know how long this journey is, nor do you know how long your life is. Get used to it and make the most of the time you have."

"On your way out you can pick up your packs," he said, pointing to three surprisingly large backpacks leaning against the side wall. "There's enough empty space for your personal effects. Inside each one is a packing list you can read tonight, as well as instructions regarding food and water. It also contains your journal," he said holding up an attractive leather-bound book. "This is your primary tool. It's for you to list the waypoints and to record lessons, questions, thoughts, plans, and anything else that becomes clear to you while you're out."

"You'll be on separate trail systems with only a small overlap at the end. Each trail terminates here at the base. Though your paths are different, you will have similar experiences and learn similar lessons. And you will all grapple with the key tenets of the *Release* process."

"The courses are set up in such a way that you don't need to hike quickly. Three to five hours of slow walking will get you from camp to camp. There's still nearly twelve hours of total daylight, so you'll have lots of time to pause, write, think, and enjoy the scenery."

"Before we break for the night, I'd like to say a prayer of blessing over you."

My head jerked up involuntarily. I hadn't anticipated anything like this, but without waiting to see if anyone had objections, Len launched into his prayer.

"God, I thank you for these people you've made for your purposes. You've created each of them with amazing abilities and stunning potential. They're here because they want to reach their full capacity for life. Please answer the craving of their hearts. Protect them during the physical, emotional, and spiritual challenges they'll face in the days ahead. Guide them through this phase of their individual journeys. Teach them what they need to learn to move into the next chapter of their lives. And help them to connect more deeply with you, their Creator. Amen."

"Amen," Shane echoed along with the staff present. Jennifer and I were both silent. Then we headed off to our rooms.

The prayer hadn't been in keeping with my spiritual beliefs, whatever they were, but I found it strangely comforting. I went to my room, packed my clothes and personal supplies, read the food and water guide, and lay in bed tired, but awake with excitement. I found myself reviewing the words Len had prayed. I realized that if I was a pray-er, it was the kind of thing I would pray that night. I wanted to reach my full potential. I wanted to know the next stage of my journey. And if indeed I had a creator, connecting more deeply with him or her or it would be a good thing, too.

"Amen." I said. My thoughts about prayer blurred into thoughts and then dreams of cougars and bears and falling from cliffs. I woke with a start several times before finally drifting into a restless, tossing sleep.

Day 3

I was already awake when Jonathon gave the wake-up calls. It was different than the previous morning: The pounding on the doors wasn't as polite, and his words were "Breakfast in five," rather than "Workout in ten."

I dressed in my hiking gear and dropped my pack on the deck before heading to the dining room. There was an air of excitement, even urgency, radiating from the staff. We were given fifteen minutes to down a simple breakfast of hot cereal, coffee, a glass of juice, and some toast. The simplicity of the meal was a great contrast to the others we'd had since arriving.

"How much are we paying for this again?" Jennifer asked, grinning when she saw the offerings.

"Enjoy it," Len said, smiling as always. "Within twenty-four hours this will seem like a feast."

When we finished eating we were immediately assigned drivers to take us to our starting points. Jennifer went with Randy, Shane with Jonathon, and I went with Marsha. The three small pickups banged down the road in the dark for several miles, almost bumper to bumper. Then Marsha suddenly veered off to the right and we were on our own.

"How far to the drop point?" I asked.

"It'll be an hour and a quarter, give or take," said Marsha. "Don't even bother trying to maintain a sense of direction."

I took her advice and dozed as much as possible, but was frequently slammed awake against the window as the tires hit rocks, potholes, and small trees lying across the road. When the vehicle finally stopped, I opened my eyes and saw we were in a small logged-off area, a "cut block" Marsha called it. The sun wasn't yet visible, but there was enough light from the northeast to see clearly. It felt cooler than the morning before, perhaps due to increased elevation.

"Turn on your GPS and get oriented," Marsha suggested, or rather ordered. She'd make a good drill sergeant I thought, resisting the temptation to mention it aloud. She unloaded my pack and stood watching as I picked up reception from the satellites. When I got a 3D reading I pushed the "page" button and the little black triangle indicating my location appeared on the screen. She told me to mark it, which I did with the push of a button. A waypoint, labeled 176, appeared. I recalled that this simply meant it was the one hundred and seventy-sixth waypoint programmed into the GPS.

"Zoom out until you see the base camp," Marsha said. It took several pushes on the "out" button before I saw a waypoint marked "base camp" appear near the lower left corner of the screen. I looked at the scale line and realized we were roughly twenty miles away "as the crow flies," perhaps twice that distance by road. Marsha handed me an index card with some coordinates printed on it.

"This is your first waypoint. I'll wait till you get it punched in and head on your way."

It took me a minute to get the waypoint location entered. Not surprisingly, the new waypoint was called 177. I paged back to the main screen and saw it scrunched against waypoint 176. I zoomed in and the waypoints separated as the scale changed. The new one looked to be no more than a mile away.

I picked up my pack, which suddenly seemed very heavy.

"Move around to determine your direction of travel toward the waypoint," said Marsha.

In a few seconds I saw that I needed to head slightly uphill toward a stand of poplars at the edge of the cut block.

"Good job!" said Marsha. "Now remember, you'll usually be walking on a trail of some kind, so your direction of travel will not always point exactly at the waypoint. Once you find a trail that heads in the right general direction, turn off your receiver to save batteries. Just check every now and then when you think you might be getting close. The first few are quite easy to navigate."

I nodded, eager to get moving in the cool morning air.

"Good luck, and God bless," said Marsha, reaching out to shake my hand.

"Thank you," I replied, not caring whether it took luck or blessing to navigate the course and reorient my life. I simply wanted results.

She hopped into the pickup, turned around, then looked back and waved before she drove out of the cut block and out of sight. In less than a minute, the noise of the vehicle faded away completely, despite the predawn calm. I was alone and I was happy, but I was also fearful of failing in my quest for personal breakthrough. I didn't know what else I could do if this trip didn't work. Strangely, I even sensed a fear that it just might work! What if I had a breakthrough? What would that mean? How would my life change? Between the wilderness context and the *Release* process I'd willingly submitted to, there were too many variables to predict or anticipate. It occurred to me that I was not in control of the outcome, and it didn't just bother me, it terrified me.

"Let's see what the day holds!" I said aloud, hoping the sound of my voice would create at least a façade of courage. Then I turned and started toward the edge of the cut.

I noticed a piece of blaze orange flagging tape on one of the poplars, and saw a well-beaten game trail heading the way I needed to go.

"This may be easier than I thought," I muttered.

After ten minutes I turned on the GPS and saw I'd covered almost half the distance to the waypoint. The game trail continued in the right direction. Another ten minutes and I was within two hundred yards. I left the receiver on as I moved closer and was still more than fifty yards away when I saw a tree with several strips of flagging tied around it. A small white box was fastened to its side. I started to run over, but remembered what Marsha had said about the danger of falling. I forced myself to slow down and arrived with my heart pounding, more from excitement than exertion. A flash of white off to my left caused me to stop abruptly, but I quickly saw it was a deer I'd startled, bounding away, tail held high in the air.

The box was made of metal and painted white. It looked like a large birdhouse and was fastened to the tree at chest height. The front had a hinged door latched shut and held with a clip like the ones on some dog leashes. I opened it and bent to look inside. Fastened to the back of the box was a laminated piece of paper with surprisingly few words written on it:

Harness your History
What are your roots — the key events and processes, good and bad, that have shaped you?

I took out my journal and copied the words at the top of the second page. I'd filled the first with random thoughts the night before.

Below the question were coordinates for the next waypoint. I copied them down, double checked them, and then programmed the GPS. I pondered the question and decided to walk for a while before writing anything down. The new waypoint was quite a bit further than the first had been, perhaps two and a half miles. But the trail I was on seemed to head the right way, so I set out.

"What are my roots...the key events and processes that have shaped me?" I asked myself as I walked along.

I began scrolling through life chronologically, beginning with my few preschool memories — a birthday party with long-forgotten playmates, a visit to my grandparents' farm where I saw a cow give birth, a terrible night when I was delirious from running a high fever and had such vivid hallucinations that my mom later told me she was scared, too.

Memories of my elementary school years became clearer. I recalled the embarrassment of vomiting in the classroom in grade one, the shocking announcement by the principle that our grade-three teacher had been killed in a car accident, and winning the first-ever school election in grade four. I recalled the long, boring summer between grades five and six when my father was hospitalized and we didn't take a planned family vacation to the west coast, but also the following summer's extended holiday in our brand new camper that more than made up for the previous year's letdown. Those five weeks in nature contained my happiest childhood memories, and I caught myself smiling. Camping in stands of large evergreens, exploring tidal flats, observing deer and moose and bears birthed in me a love of the outdoors that I sadly realized I had not cultivated for most of my adult life.

My high school years were a mix of pleasant and unpleasant experiences, which I suspected would be true for most people. Good marks, bad marks...good dates, bad dates...a little beer, and a little pot. I remembered the close friendships I'd had in those years, especially on the basketball team, and shook my head when I realized how many of those guys I hadn't seen since grad night. I thought sadly of our point guard Ted who died suddenly of an aneurism only three weeks later.

University was a grown-up version of high school with the added pressure of tuition payments, though the bike shop had easily carried me. I'd done much better academically than in high school, but had been unable to make the highly competitive basketball team. I settled for cross-country running, mostly to stay in shape.

Life since then had been mostly good, though not exciting, apart from the stocks. My jaw clenched as I remembered a previous girlfriend dumping me for a mutual acquaintance. "Please don't take it personally," she'd said. "I hope we can stay friends." Yeah, right. I still regretted the way I'd spilled my guts to her during our time together and resented the fact that she carried so many of my secrets. Even three years into my current relationship, with the woman I was sure I'd marry, I found it difficult to share with the same level of vulnerability.

The sun was now fully up and the air was warming. I stripped off my red-checkered wool jacket, purchased especially for the adventure, and stuffed it in the top of my pack. I noticed that I was walking through an old burn with charred trees, some still standing, some blown over exposing webs of roots and dirt. Roots. What were my roots? Were bad events roots? I'd certainly been shaped by unpleasant "events and processes" as well as positive ones. It just seemed odd to think of bad things as roots.

I turned on the GPS and saw that I was about three quarters of the way to the new waypoint, but I seemed to have drifted off to the right. I decided to leave the receiver on and look for a fork in the path. After a few minutes an all-terrain vehicle, or ATV, trail crossed at right angles and headed down to the left. I began following it and saw that it was bringing me directly to the waypoint. Soon, I saw a large, charred pine tree, much larger than the others in the area, with the tell-tale flagging fastened to some branches. I estimated it was about six feet in circumference, but when I tried to reach around the trunk, realized it must be more than twice that. On the far side of it was the box, which I opened and again stooped slightly to read the note it contained:

What do you learn from this tree?

What?! What do I learn from this tree? I looked around and saw a stump about twenty feet to the left, chain-sawed flat, perfect for sitting. I went and sat down, wondering if I should write out my answers to the first question before considering this new one. I decided to deal with the tree question first, since it seemed fairly simple.

I wrote down the question and looked up and down the old tree. Its top was broken off perhaps sixty feet up. The roots were partly exposed for several yards in all directions, and it looked like it had been dead for quite some time. Then I noticed something.

"Son of a gun!" I said.

Right near the top was a patch of green. I took out my binoculars and saw several small branches clustered together, some bearing cones. They couldn't have been more than a year or two old judging by their size. The old thing was alive! Its roots were still drawing moisture and nutrients from the soil, and the vascular system was moving those essentials several stories up to the small green outpost of life. I realized that since there were cones, this charred piece of timber was yet going to reproduce.

"What do you learn from this tree!" I nearly shouted the words. I could almost feel the synapses firing as my mind came to life. I found my journal and began writing, first slowly, and then as fast as I could while still keeping my script legible. Lesson after lesson, application after application broke into my consciousness. I thought of parallels between the tree and my life. I thought of friends and family members who had made small or great comebacks in marriage, finance, work, and sport. I thought of my country that sometimes seemed like an old charred tree, but which continually gave reason for hope and produced new seeds, new generations of greatness. My mind raced through applications to economics, politics, global issues, the past, and the future. I roughly sketched what the tree looked like, wishing I had a green pencil to shade in the few living branches.

I was breathless, and a little stunned, when the thoughts slowed and finally stopped. Was the question really that profound? Or was I just in a new and different head space? Was I more receptive, observant, and insightful than usual? Or had I simply created room for my heart and mind to merge?

I walked back to the tree and jotted down the new coordinates. When I entered them in the GPS and looked at the map, I saw that the new point was even further than the last segment had been, five or six miles, maybe more.

"Well," I thought, "I've got plenty of time to think and write out my answers to the first question." I opened my journal and read it again: "What are your roots — the key events and processes, good and bad, that have shaped you?"

The trail continued down with occasional wide sweeps around steep drops and thick timber. I thought suddenly and briefly about predators, but was so consumed with my thoughts of roots that fear didn't have time to settle in my mind. I walked slowly and stopped frequently to write my responses. I wished for my little digital voice recorder to speed things up, but realized it was probably helpful to document the journey in my own hand.

I checked the GPS and concluded that the trail would bring me very close to the waypoint. I stopped for a lunch break around 11:30. It was a tasty meal of salami sandwiches and baby carrots that Andrea had packed. I thought of the others for the first time, wondering if they had seen a tree similar to mine, and, if not, what question they were currently grappling with.

I was now within two miles of the waypoint, which I suspected was the camp, so I sat and wrote out everything I could think of in response to the "roots" question. When I was done, I'd filled more than eight pages with semi-legible writing. I was trying hard to keep it neat, but doubted that my thirty-plus years of lousy penmanship would change on this trip. I hoped fine script wasn't a prerequisite for "releasing my full potential." I wrote down every life-shaping event I could possibly recall, and was surprised by the things that had come to mind: A neighbor whose window I'd accidentally shot out with a sling-shot, who promised not to tell my dad as long as he never saw me shooting again; my first kiss in grade three, compliments of the cute freckle-faced girl who always sat near me; a terrifying twenty minutes one Saturday morning when I'd gotten up and couldn't find my parents, who were visiting across the street. This is amazing, I thought. The right question sure seems to get the brain working.

The ground leveled as I drew closer to the waypoint. A grouse flushed noisily from a patch of willows, causing my pulse to jump momentarily. Then I saw a log structure through the trees. I'd arrived at my first camp.

The cabin was much smaller than I'd expected, no more than six feet wide, ten feet long, and barely five feet high. I smiled and thought the cabin looked like an outhouse turned on its side. It had no windows. A thick door was latched with a clip just like the waypoint boxes. Inside, a propane lantern hung from a wire off the ridge pole, and a one-burner propane stove with a small pot sat on a rugged little table, along with a wash basin and a pump bottle of soap. Matches were in a metal canister on a plank shelf. Nailed to the back wall was the now-familiar white metal box containing my next waypoint. The bed was simply a folding army cot, and there was a small chair in the corner opposite the bed. I had no fear of predators getting into the little fortress.

I dropped my pack on the bed and walked back outside into the light. There was a pole a bit better than knee height fastened between two trees fifty feet behind the cabin. A piece of cardboard, with edges chewed by rodents, was tacked to the pole and hung down to the ground: "So you don't pee in your boots!" Randy had explained during the orientation. It was an outhouse, without the house. About fifty yards further down the trail a small stream cut through the path. It looked clean and I was tempted to drink, but we'd been instructed to boil all water except from designated locations.

After wandering around listening to the birds and watching some chipmunks stuffing their cheeks, I returned to the cabin, unpacked my sleeping bag, and napped on the cot. I woke up nearly an hour later, groggy and hungry, with a new stiffness in my shoulders from the pack.

The food and water guide instructed me to fill the pot with water from the creek, boil it for ten minutes and then add a dried potato, meat and vegetable mix from a dinner bag.

The meal was about what I expected, filling but bland. I washed the stew residue from the pot in the creek and then made some tea, heating a little extra water for the washbasin to give my face a good scrub.

I moved the chair outside and sat thinking and writing as daylight faded. A few more "root" memories, mostly positive ones now, were floating into my head. I could almost feel the heat of the bonfire and taste the hot chocolate from a family New Year's Eve party where we'd skated on a frozen pond. I wondered why the first wave of memories had been predominantly negative. Was it my personality, or were my shaping, root experiences simply negative?

I thought of another lesson from the tree, not as subtle as some had been, but still potentially powerful: A small community in my area had recently been devastated by fire, but a handful of the original pioneer families was determined to rebuild. A friend's parents were among them, and I made a note to pass on the story of the tree.

When it got too dark to see my journal, I moved inside and lit the lamp. I dug out the two-way radio, turned it on, and went through a very specific drill we'd been taught.

I gave my name and said, "Check in from Camp 1." Then I repeated it and waited.

About fifteen seconds later a voice, Andrea's I thought, repeated my words and added, "Copy that. Good night."

I would've liked to chat a bit, but we'd been told that apart from the check-in routine of names and locations, there would be no conversation except in an emergency. I flopped down on my sleeping bag, and after lying on my back staring at the ceiling for half-an-hour trying to guess what lay ahead, I decided to turn off the lamp. Despite my earlier nap, I fell asleep quickly.

Day 4

B y the time I stumbled out of the cabin the sun was breaking through the trees, but it was still cool.

"If there were windows in this cabin, I would've woken earlier," I thought. But I knew it didn't really matter. If the previous day was any indication, there was plenty of time to get where I needed to go.

I boiled a pot of water from the stream for several minutes, and then added some of it to the breakfast mixture in my bowl. As far as I could tell, the mix was oatmeal, powdered milk, and raisins. I was surprised by the size of the serving. I normally wouldn't eat so much for breakfast, but decided I better get it down as fuel for the day ahead. When I was done eating, I used the extra water to wash up and refill my water bottles.

The first waypoint was only about a mile-and-a-half away. It looked like the trail was still going in the right direction, so I stayed on it. Before long I could see a narrow but deep valley to my left through the trees. The trail seemed to be following a ridge. Three rabbits sunning on the trail ran off when I approached, and I twice heard what I assumed, and hoped, were deer running away from me.

I spotted the waypoint box easily, but when I walked up to it was startled to find myself inside what looked like a very old, very small graveyard. There were two small rotting crosses still standing, and several others fallen down. Each of the dozen or so graves was heaped with rocks. Trees grew between and out of the graves. There was nothing written on the crosses to indicate who was buried there. I thought perhaps there'd been a small settlement nearby years ago. I made a note to ask about it back at the base.

The box contained the familiar laminated paper fastened to the back. In addition to the next waypoint's coordinates were these words:

Harness Your History:
Process Your Pain
How has suffering shaped you?

It was an unsettling question in an unpleasant location. The joy of a new day began to fade as I copied the question and coordinates into my notebook. I walked back to the trail and found a comfortable place where I could sit in the sun and see the valley through the trees.

"This might take a while," I thought.

I flipped back to my answers from the day before, reviewing "the key events and processes" of my life. Many fit the category of "suffering." I copied them over onto my new page. As I did, other painful events surfaced in my mind. I was surprised both by their vividness and by the immediate emotional impact they elicited. It was like my senses had been heightened by the silence and solitude. Listing the memories was the easy part. But the question I now needed to grapple with was, "How has this suffering shaped me?"

It didn't take long to trace how the relatively minor sufferings of my pre-teen and early teen years had gradually, but permanently, eroded my sense of innocence and the delusion that the world was a friendly, safe place. Growing older, various relationships I'd experienced and observed had shattered my trust in people. I approached most professional and personal interactions with involuntary suspicion. Health struggles in my mid-twenties made me realize I was mortal and would one day die. "If you were forty, we'd be firing a pacemaker into you!" the doctor had said. "And besides the erratic heart beat, you've got a leaky valve. Probably need a valve job before you're sixty!" Like a lot of specialists, I guessed this one had flunked "Bedside Sensitivity" class. I suddenly realized that the high level of fitness I worked to maintain was tied to the fear his diagnosis had planted in me. The death of my father a few years earlier had underscored this sense of mortality. It was a final thrust out of the youth I'd desperately clung to, and into the realization that I was an aging adult and would be until I died.

I was exhausted when I finished writing ninety minutes later. I now believed that suffering had shaped me more than I'd known, and certainly more than I wanted. In fact, it seemed like suffering and pain were the most significant shaping processes of my life. Difficult events seemed to define so much of my personality, preferences, ideals, and beliefs.

My head was as full of memories as my heart was of emotions, few of them pleasant, as I stood and moved slowly toward the new coordinates. How was it possible to feel so lousy on such a great day? In my emotional fog I nearly stepped into a big mound of black, berry-filled dung. It was bear scat, exactly as Marsha had described it. I fingered my bear spray and looked around with mild concern. I gave a couple yells just to let any resident bears know a human was in the neighborhood. I hoped Marsha was right when she said that wilderness bears generally harbor a healthy fear of people.

At a mud hole made by a small watercourse, I checked the GPS and realized the waypoint was almost directly to my right. No trail was visible. I decided to head straight toward where my GPS indicated, since it was only about a hundred and fifty yards away.

The white box was nailed to a tree right beside a hole in the ground from which clear water bubbled. I concluded that the spring was the cause of the mud hole on the trail, and when I opened the box was delighted to read:

Drink your fill and fill your water bottles!

I obeyed immediately. The water was so cold it made my teeth ache. But it felt good all the way down, and pushed my uncomfortable emotions slightly into the background. When my water bottles and I were fully saturated, I turned my attention to the other instructions:

Harness Your History:
Process Your Pain
Allow your pain to impact you,
but not define you.

48

The profundity of the statement hit me even before I finished transferring the words to my journal. Over the last few uncomfortable hours, I'd allowed my pain to define me. I'd even been wallowing in it. I realized, with some shock, that I'd also been doing so unconsciously, in a more concealed way, for most of my adult life. Ironically, my fear of being impacted by pain had led me to ignore it, bury it, and not deal with it at all. The final result: It had in some ways defined me! I wrote down a fresh thought that flashed into my mind: "Unless I allow my pain to impact me appropriately, it WILL define me. I accept the impact, but I refuse to be defined by my pain."

As I worked my way through the tangle back to the trail, my spirit lifted. It was the birth of what, over the next few months, would become an unusual freedom I'd never known before — a freedom to feel pain, to allow it to impact me, but to fend, even laugh off the suggestion that I was in any way defined or limited or excused by the pain I'd experienced.

The sun floated higher and I felt better as I moved down the trail. I could see the valley to the east more clearly as the trees on the ridge grew sparse and the trail moved closer to the edge. It was not a wide valley, but it was very deep, full of thick vegetation. Far below through the trees I could hear the rush of water. I was glad to be up top and not down below.

Lunch was "gorp," a mix of nuts, dried fruit, and chocolate chips. It tasted great and made me thirsty, but I didn't mind, now that I had lots of good water. I chose to munch on the gorp as I walked along. There was a light breeze on the exposed ridge, so I put my wool jacket back on.

The ridge dropped a bit, then leveled off. The valley was still visible to my left and had begun to broaden considerably.

The trees grew thicker on my right, but the relative absence of undergrowth made it feel like a city park. I was pleased to discover my cabin just down off the ridge, nestled in the big timber. I calculated that I'd walked seven or eight miles through the day.

The white box in the cabin contained some surprises. Surprise number one was that I would spend two nights at the camp. An envelope was labeled, "Coordinates for Day 6: Do not open until then!" Surprise number two was another envelope labeled, "Debrief notes for Day 4: Processing Your Pain." Another envelope said, "Debrief Notes for Day 5." There was also a large steel box containing food for my stay, as well as some supplies for the next leg of the journey. The cabin was otherwise equipped much as the first one had been, but also contained a folding lawn chair which I promptly carried up the ridge where I could look over the valley while I read through the Day 4 debrief. It was a letter from Len.

Dear Release Adventurer,

Congratulations on your progress so far — physically, emotionally, and spiritually.

You may have found today emotionally difficult. Please remember that your pain need not define you. Indeed, it cannot do so unless you allow it to. However, it is important for you to know that some pain you have faced might require wise, outside counsel. It may be too slow and difficult to process on your own.

In more than twenty years of studying and practicing leadership, I've discovered that most high achievers, in fact every one of them I know personally, has been in some kind of counseling or therapy. Why? Because all high achievers I know personally have experienced significant pain. But instead of being destroyed by it, they've come to grips with their brokenness, learned some key life lessons from the hurt, and moved on. They've dealt with their "stuff." That is also what you must do.

Pain is a part of life. I will face pain. You will face pain. It is what we do with the pain that determines whether it is ultimately debilitating and destructive, or contributes to who we can ideally become. Surprisingly, pain is part of the raw material that contributes to the release of our full potential.

This is the most important step in Harnessing Your History. You will have opportunity to talk to someone about this when you arrive back at the base. But for now, why not write out a prayer to whomever or whatever you believe God to be? Talk about your most significant experiences of pain and suffering, and ask for help. Whether you choose to do this or not, please decide now that you will not walk through your pain alone.

Press on!
Sincerely, your fellow traveler,
Len

I could hear Len's voice in the words of the letter. His sincerity seeped through. I decided that I would indeed talk to someone back at the base about certain aspects of my pain, especially how past hurts had unconsciously shaped my behavior. I'd identified a few cases where this seemed to have happened, and I wanted to learn how to recognize other instances of this pattern. Len's comments about high achievers getting counsel surprised me.

I wondered if I should seek further therapy. And what the heck, I thought, I'll write out a prayer to God.

The prayer was difficult and awkward at first. Why was I so self-conscious out there all alone? But the more I wrote, the easier it flowed. At times I stopped writing and simply talked out loud. It was like speaking with someone in whom I had total trust. Eventually, my guard dropped completely, and I said things I'd never told anyone and had rarely even admitted to myself. I was surprised by how significant a factor fear seemed to be in my life — fear of failure, but more surprisingly, fear of success! It seemed to be tied to the emptiness I'd felt at every significant milestone in my life. The accomplishment of my goals had never brought the deep satisfaction I'd longed for, so even success had somehow added to my pain. Lately, it seemed, the dull ache actually began before the accomplishments, in anticipation of the impending disappointment.

"So, I guess I could use some help breaking out of this routine," I wrote in conclusion.

I understood the psychological benefits of catharsis, but this seemed like something more. I found it odd how writing and speaking out a request for help, to a being whose existence I was unsure of, seemed to stir life deep in my soul.

I walked back to the camp and turned my attention to supper. The steel food box gave me multiple options. I ate some peanut butter and honey with crackers while I sorted through the possibilities. I settled on macaroni and cheese with a can of cream corn — not a meal I would normally cook, but it seemed to match my cravings. I washed it down with a can of vegetable juice, and had more crackers and honey for dessert. I sealed up the garbage in a plastic container as instructed, and put it back in the steel box. I realized I'd forgotten to make the call to base camp, and did so quickly, with results identical to the first day, only this time I didn't mind the ban on conversation and was quite happy to turn the radio off and return to my thoughts.

I walked back up the ridge with my journal. The shadows lengthened as the sun set. I wrote and watched as the light on the east valley wall dimmed and grew dark. Just before it was too black to walk safely, I picked up the lawn chair and returned to the cabin. I lit the lamp and sipped some herbal tea until I felt totally relaxed. Then I killed the light and slowly drifted off, feeling freer and lighter, better equipped to live.

Day 5

A woodpecker banging on a nearby tree woke me earlier than I wanted, but the sense of peace and refreshment I'd tasted the evening before still remained. Breakfast was pancakes fried in olive oil from a small sealed bottle in the grub box. There was syrup, but no butter. I used some milk powder to make a glass of milk, my drink of choice with pancakes. A little fresh fruit or some fried eggs, and breakfast would've been perfect.

After I wrote down the coordinates and entered them in my GPS, I packed a lunch of peanut butter and honey smeared on crackers, some fruit juice, and a cup of gorp. There were food containers labeled, "Take on Day 6," but even without them there was a clear surplus of food for my two nights on the ridge. The coordinate sheet indicated there was no obvious trail to my destination, which bothered me slightly as I recalled the bear scat from the day before. I didn't relish the thought of pushing through the bush with low visibility. The good news was that the waypoint looked to be less than two miles away.

"That's far enough without a trail," I thought, "But certainly doable."

I put my journal, food, and water in the detachable day pack which was part of the larger framed backpack. It would feel good walking without the full load.

The parkland pine grove offered easy walking for the first half mile. A pair of grouse flushed out of a bush just as I set out, giving me a start. The trees grew smaller, the ground began to slope upward, and increasing underbrush made walking difficult. I checked my receiver frequently to make sure I was tracking properly. At one point the ground sloped up so steeply that I had to climb with my hands. Large boulders forced me into a zigzag path, and I was surprised by how winded I felt. Eventually, I broke through to a clearing that allowed me to look back the way I'd come. It was spectacular.

The sun was about halfway to lunch time, just high enough to allow me to look back to the east without shielding my eyes. The rise I'd just climbed was simply a higher edge to the valley I'd walked along and looked over the day before. I couldn't see the cabin through the trees, but recognized the sharp drop beyond where it was, down to the river below. A thin strip of mist rose from the lowest part of the valley. To the south it widened and was joined by two larger troughs coming from the east and the southwest, forming a large basin. The trees were a thick green blanket, and there was no sign of human activity except for some distant cut blocks and a quickly fading jet trail in the sky. I saw a hawk drifting along enjoying the morning with me. A squirrel chattered to my left. It was a fine day to be alive.

I took a few draughts of water while I caught my breath. According to the GPS I was about half a mile from my destination. It looked like I would have to go over the top and down the other side, angling to the northwest.

When I began my descent I was immediately in the shade and the forest changed dramatically. The trees were tight; many had died and partially fallen, but were being held up by others. I pushed my way through the intertwined branches and stepped over logs that had made it only partway to the ground. When I tried to check my progress, the receiver couldn't get reception through the trees. I just kept heading down in what I felt was the right direction until a small clearing allowed me to get a reading. I saw that I was far enough down the slope, but needed to head three hundred yards north along the side of the hill. I wondered what on earth I was looking for.

I hadn't gone two hundred yards more when the bush suddenly thinned and ended. A cliff ran above me parallel to my line of travel and a slope of rocks and boulders cascaded down to my left. I checked my GPS and saw that I needed to head right for the cliff.

"What am I looking for?" I asked myself out loud.

As I drew close, I saw a hole right at the base of the cliff, timbers bracing its top and sides. A long wooden trough ran down the slope. What looked like a very small rail car lay on its side near the hole. It was a mine shaft. I reasoned that the trough must be an old sluice box. A small amount of water, about the volume that would come from a half-open garden hose, flowed from the old mine and disappeared into the rocks below. I didn't see the white box immediately, but when I got to the mouth of the hole, there it was, nailed just inside to one of the timbers.

Also hanging from the timbers was a small shovel and a green plastic pan I was sure must be a gold pan. I guessed I might be doing some mining.

I opened the box with great interest. There were no coordinates on the laminated sheet since I was simply returning to camp that night. All it said was:

Harness your History:
Embrace Your Encouragement
Pan some Gold!
PS: You can drink this water!

On the bottom of the box was a little laminated pamphlet explaining how to pan for gold. In the dim light I almost didn't notice a postcard-sized envelope that directed me to open it when I found some gold.

I read the instructions and set to work. I took a spade full of gravel from a pool of water just outside the mouth of the mine and dumped it in the pan. I shook it vigorously, keeping it covered with water, then fished out the larger stones. I started swirling it in a circle to achieve what the pamphlet called "liquid suspension," which would allow the heavier metals to sink to the bottom. Then I tilted the pan, shaking it back and forth, allowing the lighter silt and stones to slide out over the riffles in the pan. The riffles were supposed to catch the heavier gold and keep it from being washed out.

After about fifteen minutes, far longer than I suspected a real miner would take, I was down to the "black sand" or magnetite which was heavier than most rock, but still lighter than gold. At this point, in keeping with the instructions, I tilted the pan back away from the riffles, and swirled the water up around the black sand, washing away small portions of it each time. When roughly one-third of the black sand had fallen back, I saw a small fleck of yellow. I felt a rush of excitement and kept swirling, eventually revealing three more tiny specks of gold. I knew the small amount of gold in the pan weighed so little it was worth almost nothing, but I had a sudden compulsion to do another pan.

I realized with disappointment that I had nothing to put the gold in. But then I had a brain wave. I opened my full water bottle, pressed a finger tip against one of the flecks of metal until it stuck, put my finger in the bottle, and washed it off. It dropped to the bottom. I did the same with the other flakes, and then set about doing another pan. This one took about half the time and produced seven flakes. The exhilaration I felt helped me understand the "gold fever" I'd heard about in old western movies and a history class. I did a third pan before remembering I had an envelope to open.

I scooped a few handfuls of the icy water from just above where I was panning and had a drink. Then I went in and got the envelope. A large rounded boulder sat off to one side of the mine and I crawled up onto it to read. The slope below was now in the sun, but it looked like my spot would be in the shade until early evening.

The paper inside the envelope said:

Harness your History:
Embrace Your Encouragement
List the things people have said or done
throughout your life to encourage you.

"That's it?" I asked. "A long uphill walk followed by a fight through the tangle just for this?"

I felt let down. The impact of the day before had been so significant that this felt anticlimactic. I opened my lunch and sat on the rock eating and thinking. I was a bit chilly now that I'd stopped moving, and wished I had my wool jacket. It was still before noon and I estimated I could get back in less than two hours, so I walked down the slope until I hit the sunshine and found another comfortable rock to use as a seat while I wrote.

I reflected on the metaphor of the day: Panning for gold... encouragement. A lot of waste rock, a few flecks of gold. And yet what a thrill when those flecks appeared!

"There might be something to this," I thought as I opened my journal and began the list of encouragements I'd received.

My grandmother was kind of a pen pal to me until I was eleven, when she died. I still had some of the letters. They were praise from one end to the other — congratulations for any little accomplishment in school, and expressions of joy over the stories I told her about my life. She snuck in small bits of advice from time to time, but they were so saturated with encouragement they just slipped down like candy-coated vitamins. It occurred to me that her praise was the foundation of my self-esteem. I didn't consider myself arrogant — though I suppose few arrogant people do — but I did have a fairly healthy ego. And it came from her.

My parents were not nearly so effusive in their praise to me or my siblings, but they had been net contributors to my self worth. I recalled a time after my second year of college when I won a major scholarship. My father drove for eleven hours to take me out for dinner to celebrate. He looked me in the eye and told me he was so proud of me, always had been, and knew I was going to have a great life. My eyes grew misty as I thought of him and missed him.

I had a basketball coach in high school who had somehow developed me from a barely third-string player into a starter. What struck me as I reflected on his role in my life, was that he'd taught me almost nothing about basketball, but had encouraged me and the others on the team constantly. I thought of the times people told me, "You're so encouraging!" and realized that at those moments I'd simply been mimicking Coach.

There were other incidents and other people, some I could capture in one line: JJ's high five when I got a promotion at work; Dave's index finger pointed at me like a gun when I made a strong point in a committee meeting; Stephanie's "Thank You"

61

card for encouraging her through a tough time. As with the pain exercise, the more I wrote the more I recalled. I wrote for roughly the same time as I had the day before, but produced twice the number of pages. My emotions were a contrast to twenty-four hours earlier, when it felt like pain was the dominant shaping factor in my life. Encouragement was beginning to challenge for that position. And unlike the day before, when I was so exhausted, I was quickly becoming energized and ready to press ahead with the journey... and with life.

I worked my way back up the slope to the mine, and did two more pans before leaving. I was surprised when the last pan yielded no gold, and made a note in my journal that sometimes, even when we are doing the right thing, there will not always be immediate reward. I returned the equipment to its original place and put the small paper back into the envelope and then the box. After filling my half-empty water bottle from the trickle in the mine, drinking, and then refilling it, I worked my way back along the rock face until I could begin to go up the slope. The tangle was not as severe as where I'd come over further to the south, and I easily crested the ridge and began down the other side.

I arrived back at the cabin around 4:30. Though the walk had been shorter in distance, it was more rigorous than the one the day before. I radioed the base and ate a few more crackers with peanut butter and honey while I decided what to do for supper. I settled on a can of processed meat, which I roasted in chunks on a stick over a fire in the pit outside. I would never eat that kind of stuff at home, but it actually tasted pretty good when it was slightly burned and dripping with juice. I also heated a small can of beans on the propane burner and downed a can of veggie juice.

After supper I didn't feel like going back up to the ridge, so I sat just outside the cabin and read the debrief notes, another letter from Len.

Dear Adventurer,

I hope you enjoyed the challenge of the day and the variety of food at your disposal!

Before you go to sleep tonight, I want to make sure you truly Embrace Your Encouragement. In some ways this is the opposite of Processing your Pain, but both must be harnessed. Just as we all have pain in our lives we must deal with, we also have encouragement in our lives we must accept if we are to reach our full potential. This is all part of gathering the raw materials needed for the chain reaction and resulting energy release.

What does "embrace" mean? It means you accept it. It means when someone honestly encourages you (not flatters you — we all know the difference), you believe it and allow it to soak in. You don't brush it off or put up a little wall in your heart to prevent it from taking root. You may know from experience what I'm talking about. You may have a hard time accepting encouragement or receiving love. In many cases this is because you have not processed your pain. But as you do, you'll find that your ability to accept, believe, and embrace encouragement, as well as your capacity to receive love, will grow. When encouragement comes your way, develop the habit of accepting it. And be sure you also generate some encouragement for the many around you who desperately need it, too.

Here's a tip: Keep an encouragement file. When you get an encouraging card or an email from someone, file it away for future reference. We all go through times in our lives when it seems like everyone and everything is saying, "You're a loser! You can't do anything right, you're a fool and nobody wants you." It isn't true, of course, but it can feel true. So when you're in one of those intense down times, pull out your encouragement file and do some reading. As you do, you'll be reminded that someone likes you, that you have done some things right, and that the truth about you doesn't correspond to how you feel at the moment. It takes a steady stream of encouragement to keep the energy release going. Embrace Your Encouragement!

Have a good sleep, you'll need it.
Press on!
Len.

I chose not to reflect on his closing line as I lay in bed writing and thinking. I held my water bottle up to the light and looked at the little specks of gold on the bottom. My thoughts oscillated between daydreaming about what it would be like to find a big nugget in the bottom of a gold pan, and my memories of encouragement over the years. Despite only having a couple dozen flakes of gold worth almost nothing by weight, I closed my eyes feeling much richer than when the day began.

Day 6

I woke slowly to the sound of a light rain. With a groan, I sat up in bed and fantasized about a hot bath and a mug of gourmet coffee. My legs were stiff from the slope the day before.

"Oh well," I thought, "Instant coffee will have to do."

While the water boiled, I opened the envelope that said "Do not open until Day 6." It contained the usual coordinates as well as a note reminding me to bring the designated food supplies.

I ate a big bowl of oatmeal with brown sugar and milk. I found myself stalling, hoping the rain would let up, but there was no indication of that happening. If anything, it was getting heavier. Reluctantly, I dug out my rain suit and packed up my gear. Adding to my reluctance was the awareness that my time at this ridge camp had been personally significant. My life had been changed in a lasting way. I closed the door, said a silent goodbye, and walked up the trail along the edge of the ridge before turning on my receiver. The visibility was very poor — I couldn't even see across the valley — and I hoped my line of travel would continue to follow the trail.

When the receiver had adequate satellite reception and kicked over to the map page, I began walking along the trail hoping the little triangle would tell me I was headed in the right direction. Instead, it showed me walking at right angles to the waypoint. I turned left off the trail and headed toward the edge of the ridge. The arrow pointed directly at my waypoint.

"This can't be right," I thought, and went through the exercise again. I dug out my notebook and tried vainly to keep it dry while I double-checked the coordinates. The ones in my book matched up with what I had on the GPS.

"Shoot!" I yelled in frustration.

It looked like my next destination was two or three miles away, right across the valley, maybe even over the top of the other side. I decided to walk the trail to the south, hoping it would wind down into the valley, but within 200 yards it simply ended in a big circle where ATVs had obviously turned around dozens of times. I considered backtracking to the north in case a trail branched off along the Day 4 segment of my walk, but I was sure I would have seen it.

Still, I wasn't convinced that going over the edge of the ridge, right across the valley, was the intended pathway. Then I remembered Len's closing on the debrief notes of the night before: "Have a good sleep, you'll need it!" I groaned out loud for the second time that day, took a deep breath, and started over the edge.

The slope was not as steep as I'd expected, but it was wet and slippery. There was no indication of a trail, so I just kept heading down the most obvious way. Several times I lost my footing and dropped to one knee, eventually bashing them both. Once I lost both feet and crashed to my side where I lay for thirty seconds before getting up. I dug out some leather work gloves I had in the pack so I could use my hands without them getting cold and shredded.

The rain continued and the slope steepened. It was mostly rock with a few little bushes and dangerous pockets of moss that slid off when I stepped on them. I realized that if the valley wall got much steeper I could easily have a serious fall. Eventually I came to the edge of a thirty-foot drop that ran both ways along the ridge. I walked first to the north and then the south trying to find a way down. In some places the drop doubled in distance, but never grew less than about thirty feet. There was no way down, not without climbing equipment. I sat down discouraged, wondering if I needed to go all the way back up and around the main ridge by some other route.

As I sat considering my options, I mindlessly watched a strip of flagging tape, tied to a tree, fluttering in the breeze. Suddenly I realized what it was and quickly got up to take a look. Then I saw more flagging marking a line to the edge of the drop. I walked forward hesitantly. My heart jumped when I saw a rope ladder, fastened to pins in the rock, dropping down over the side. It was a welcome shot of joy in what had so far been a miserable morning.

The good news was that I'd found the way down. The bad news was that it was a rope ladder over the lip of a potentially fatal drop on a rainy day, and I had to make it with all my gear.

"I guess this is what waivers are for," I thought as I moved into position.

The ladder began well before it was actually needed, but I kept my hand on it anyway. When it actually dropped over the edge, I had to wiggle and fight to get my feet on each rung while I kept a death grip on the higher rungs with my gloved hands. Once I was over the lip it got easier. Every three or four feet the sides of the rope ladder were anchored into spikes in the rock, keeping it from swinging.

The climb down seemed to take forever, but I think it was only about five minutes before my feet finally touched solid ground and I let out a relieved breath that hung for a second in the cold air. I took a drink from one of my water bottles, more as an excuse to rest than to quench thirst. Just a stone's throw below me, the forest began again and I hoped the worst was over. I checked my bearing and continued down into the trees.

In a few minutes I found myself in some of the biggest timber I'd seen so far — not as big as the big tree on Day 3, but on average much larger than anything else along the trail. Unfortunately, many smaller trees and some of the larger ones had fallen. Crawling over and under them quickly made me muddy and sweaty, and I ripped my new, expensive rain suit in several places on the broken branches of the downed trees.

After an hour or so of slow, struggling progress, I finally reached the creek. I'd been unsure what to expect, remembering the noise of rushing water I'd heard from the ridge two days before. The creek was about thirty feet across, filled with foaming water tumbling over rocks. I didn't think I could safely walk through the flow, so I worked my way to the left looking for some way of crossing. I was hoping for a bridge, but what I got was a rope tied to a large tree on each side, looping down almost touching the water in the middle of the creek. I realized with my third groan of the day that I was supposed to wade the creek hanging onto the rope.

Without the rope it would have been a dangerous crossing, and even with the help it was difficult keeping my feet under me. It was also numbingly cold. I sloshed out of the water on the other side, wet to my waist and shivering. I took off my boots and changed my socks in keeping with advice Marsha had given "in case we ever got very wet feet." She knew perfectly well I was going to get wet feet! I wondered what kind of equivalent day the others were having, doubting it could be less fun than this.

Sometime during the morning the rain lightened and stopped, though it was hard to tell with all the water dripping from the trees. I found a relatively dry place under the mantel of a large spruce and had lunch. A thermos of good hot chocolate would have been worth a lot of money to me at that moment. I decided to get going quickly before I chilled.

At first it seemed that the same mess of timber continued beyond the creek. But as the ground started to slope upward, the trees grew smaller and I noticed little game trails crisscrossing through the underbrush. Whenever I found one that seemed to be going in the right direction I'd follow it until it veered off the correct line of travel. Then I'd take another reading and walk directly toward the waypoint until I crossed another hopeful trail.

This worked well for half an hour or so, but then the slope increased and the trees grew smaller and tighter. It soon became almost identical to the bush near the mine the day before.

69

The branches from each tree intertwined with the next. Dead-falls interrupted my progress every few feet. In frustration, I often tried to bulldoze my way forward through the soaking brush, only to scratch my face and tear my rain suit further. I stopped frequently to catch my breath.

It was 2:30 when the ground began to level and the trees opened up. A reading told me I was less than a mile from my destination, so I took off my tattered rain suit, packed it away, and made a beeline for the camp.

It was easy walking, and before I had time to fully enjoy being out of the ugly bush I saw the cabin in the middle of a clearing. A nice trail headed off to the south. Though the rain had stopped and the sky was still heavily overcast, I smiled when I opened the cabin door and dumped my soggy gear on the floor.

The first thing I did was radio the base camp. I figured they'd be glad to know they didn't have to send a search party into the maze I'd pushed through all day.

When I said my check-in piece, Andrea gave her usual response but added, "Congratulations on surviving Day 6!"

"Thanks," I said with some pride, wanting to talk more and complain a bit and brag some, but knowing it would have to wait.

I heated some water for tea and spread out my clothes to dry while I enjoyed the warmth of clean underwear, another pair of dry socks, and my wool jacket. I missed my girlfriend, wishing I could tell her some of the things I was learning, and also daydreamed about how good it would feel to snuggle up to her warmth after a day like I'd just had. I was curious about the lesson of the day, so I snapped out of my imagination, went to the white box, and read the laminated paper on the back:

Harness Your History:
Admit Your Ability!
List the things you do better than most people, and the character traits you have that make you unique.

As usual, the coordinates for the next day were printed underneath the words. There was also a debrief note for the day and a sealed envelope with the odd inscription, "Open at precisely 2 pm, Day 7." I held it up to the light to see if I could read anything inside, but nothing was visible. When the tea water was ready I made a cup and sat down to read Len's letter.

Dear Tired and Hungry Adventurer,

If you are reading this, you must have survived Day 6! Good job. If I was there I would shake your hand, give you a big hug, and cook you dinner. Simply completing this day indicates some significant ability and depth of character. In fact, one week ago, could you have done it?

I paused and thought about his question. One week ago I would not have survived such a day. I didn't know how to use a GPS, I would've been extremely uncomfortable in the wilderness alone, and it would've been very dangerous for me to attempt such a traverse. Not that it wasn't dangerous now, but I had some new knowledge and had tapped some inner resources I was unaware of a mere seven days earlier. I continued with his letter.

This is the essence of Release — hidden abilities and possibilities within you that need to be released. And you're only partway through your journey! Please take the application exercise for today very seriously. Take your time and leave space in your journal for new thoughts that come to mind over the next several days. To make the exercise more concrete, think of significant accomplishments you've had and the skills and character qualities those accomplishments indicate. And be sure to add the list you develop to the Encouragement File I hope you will begin when you get home.

Some people have great difficulty with this exercise. When asked to make a list of their weaknesses and faults, they can rattle off item after item. But when asked about their strengths, they freeze up and get uncomfortable, feeling unworthy. If this describes you, fight through it. Today proves you have some amazing potential! Identify it and begin to release it. The abilities you uncover will lead to ideas for future direction. Like GPS coordinates, they will show you where to pinpoint your efforts. Maximum energy release comes when we focus on things in which we can excel, because these things tap into the core of who we are and how we're wired.

Enjoy your sleep tonight, along with the treat in your food pack.
Press on!
Len

I quickly jumped up and dug out the food supplies I'd picked up at the last cabin. I found a small package wrapped in brown paper, taped shut. When I opened it I was thrilled to find three of my favorite chocolate bars and a can of pop. I wondered if they somehow knew these were my favorite bars, or if it was simply a fluke. I enjoyed one right away with my tea, and had one later for dessert.

Before it was time to prepare my evening meal, I began the exercise and slowly developed a substantial list of my abilities. In some areas it overlapped with the encouragements from the day before, but there were other significant things I'd done that no one else knew about, and so had never acknowledged. I felt my self assurance and pride rising moment by moment as I listed accomplishments, skills, and character traits. The last two days had produced a huge ego boost, a sudden inflow of self esteem. Len had been dead right back on the opening night. This was not a false or exaggerated way of boosting our self image. It was based on what had become, through the questions and reflection, self-evident truth. That's why it had such power. I knew the things I listed were true, and no one could've convinced me otherwise.

After supper I listed some more observations, reread my notes from the very beginning, and added a few more thoughts. I turned the lights out not long after the hidden sun had set, and fell into a comfortable, deep, warm sleep.

Day 7

I woke just after 5:00 am and for about forty-five minutes tried to get back to sleep. Finally I gave up and rose to meet the rising sun. The clouds were gone and it was promising to be a fabulous day. I felt totally in control. My pride and sense of accomplishment from the day before were still strong.

I ate more quickly than usual, eager to get on with the day just in case rain moved in again. My goal was to be at the new camp well before 2:00 pm, when I was supposed to open the sealed envelope. Some of my clothes and my boots were still damp, and I hoped that if I got to the camp early I could finish drying them out.

The new waypoint was further east, forming a nearly straight line on the receiver's screen with my present location and the cabin from nights four and five. That made me nervous: I'd quickly learned there was no such thing as a straight line on the journey. I hoped the trail to the south curved east where I needed to go.

The birds sounded happy and I was happy as I headed down the trail. After about a mile I checked the GPS and saw that the path was still heading south. I followed it for another twenty minutes. When it veered to the west instead of the east like I needed, I knew I had to make a decision: Should I head back to the cabin and go toward the waypoint from there? Or should I simply strike out from my current location?

I hated to go back the same way I'd already come. Even at home in civilization when I went on a trip, I wouldn't backtrack one block unless I'd forgotten something very important, like my wallet. I paused and reflected on my larger life journey: Was there a right way and a wrong way to get to the same place? Or was simply arriving at the destination the crucial factor?

It didn't look like there was much difference in the distance I'd have to travel either way, so I opted to shoot for the waypoint from where I was. It looked less than three miles away, so after a quick drink and a handful of gorp I was off.

The walking was easy compared to the tangles I'd been through the last two days. I saw several grouse and there seemed to be squirrels everywhere. I again heard something large running off into the brush, but didn't catch a glimpse of it.

The ground sloped gradually uphill for three-quarters of a mile before heading downward. Walking was still quite easy, with only the odd string of thicker brush. The sun was warm and there was almost no wind. I rarely checked the receiver, but simply kept the sun in my face. I knew it would be moving to my right in the sky, but not fast enough to matter over such a short distance.

I heard the river before I saw it. Its roar filled the valley to the north and the south. The closer I got, the steeper the valley wall grew, until it leveled out for the last 200 yards to the water. And it was indeed a river, not a creek, at least forty feet across, water raging. My waypoint was tantalizingly close, no more than 500 yards, but the river stood in my way. I wondered what Len and his people had constructed to allow people to cross. I momentarily regretted my decision not to backtrack, thinking that if I'd traveled straight from the cabin I might have hit the river in exactly the right spot. I had no idea if I was upstream or downstream from the crossing. I took a sip of water and mentally flipped a coin: Should I go upstream or downstream? There was a path running along the river bank both ways. I decided to head downstream.

The walking was easy, but I couldn't hear a thing because of the river. This was one of the dangerous situations Marsha had warned us about. Usually a bear will run if it knows a person is near, but if it doesn't know you are there and you surprise it... well, all bets are off. I made sure my bear spray was handy.

The river frothed and sprayed the entire way down, and then after fifteen minutes it suddenly dropped off into a roaring waterfall I hadn't heard due to the river noise around me. The trail stayed well back from the edge and veered right. I pushed through some trees and walked out toward the top of the falls as far as was safe. Mist rose from the roar as water smashed into rocks more than fifty feet below. I knew that if this spot was accessible by road it would be a tourist attraction. I wondered how many hidden places like this there were in the world that few, if any, people ever saw. The view was both captivating and invigorating. As I took several deep breaths trying to internalize the wonder of the moment, I realized that this was one of the many rich experiences I wouldn't have tasted if I'd never started the journey. Marsha's words from Day 2 came to mind: "It's better to die on a quest to reach your full potential than to never start the journey." When she'd first said them, I wasn't sure if they were true or not, but I now found myself in full agreement.

From my vantage point I could see the river flowing downstream for at least another half mile before it curved. I dug out my binoculars and scanned up and down both sides and right up the middle of the river in case there was a rope bridge or some other structure spanning the water, but I saw nothing. I concluded that the crossing must be upstream from where I began.

It was nearly lunchtime, so I decided to enjoy the view and eat up on the ledge in the sun. I inhaled my remaining chocolate bar first, proving that I still lacked self control, sipped on fruit juice, and had some tasty, dried, flavored meat called "jerky." I was still hoping to get to camp before my self-imposed 2:00 pm deadline, so I walked quickly back the way I'd come. I recognized the place where I'd first approached the river, and walked with increasing excitement. I knew the bridge had to be close.

Thirty minutes later there was still no bridge. The water was a torrent the entire way, with no spot even remotely safe to cross. I walked more slowly for another thirty minutes and saw nothing that helped me. I checked my GPS and saw I was significantly north of the waypoint. I was getting irritated!

"Maybe I'm supposed to get across somehow by myself, without a bridge," I thought.

But how? I had no rope, and even if I had, what good would it have done? I thought about chopping down one of the large trees that leaned out over the river, but if that was the requirement, surely there would be evidence that others had done the same thing. I couldn't see Len and his team allowing a large tree to be knocked down every time someone came on the course. Besides, with the little hatchet in my pack it would take an entire day to fall any tree large enough to cross the river.

I was so sure I hadn't missed the crossing point that I kept walking for another half hour. Maybe the river had washed out whatever had been in place? I didn't think so — it was too late in the year for high water, and others had been on this same course within the last few weeks.

At 1:30 I gave up and sat down on a log. There wasn't a lot of sun getting through the large trees, but I found a sliver of light and settled down to wait until 2:00 when I could open the envelope. I hoped it would tell me what I had to do to cross. Perhaps there was some hidden equipment on my side that I could use, though I couldn't imagine what that equipment might be.

I dozed off until my watch signaled 2:00. The envelope was waiting in my hand and I tore it open. When I read it I swore out loud.

Harness Your History:
Live Within Your Limits
There is no way for you to cross this river.
Go back and stay another night at the cabin.

I stared at the paper in disbelief and swore again, anger tightening my chest. I'd been walking for hours, looking desperately for

79

something that didn't exist! I realized there was no waypoint on the other side, just some inaccessible coordinates designed to challenge and frustrate me. A rage rose up from deep inside me, a rage that I'm sure colored my face as I spat out a string of profanity unlike anything I'd ever uttered.

At the bottom of the note were the numbers for the next day as well as the words, "Check this out on your way back," and another set of numbers. When I entered them in the receiver with my shaking hand, a waypoint showed up only a few hundred yards from the cabin.

I started marching back with a smoldering fury. The sky was blue, the wind was light, and I was ready to kill. For someone who hated to backtrack, this was the worst possible scenario.

"There better be something great at the waypoint by the cabin," I muttered. "Like a hot tub, or a gold nugget, or at least another chocolate bar."

Fortunately, it was an easy walk, and I quickly entertained then discarded the idea of quitting. I got to the waypoint by 3:00, opened the white box and pulled out a can of pop, the sight of which gave my spirits a boost. There was also an envelope with my name on it, another letter from Len, I expected.

"It better be a good one," I thought.

I didn't open it until I got back to the cabin, took off my boots, dragged the chair outside, sat down, and cracked open the drink. The letter began:

I am almost tempted to offer an apology.

"You should!" I said.

But I won't. Like most of the high-performance people we deal with, you are likely very unaware of your limits. Ironically, if you are going to experience maximum energy release and reach your full potential, this needs to change.

Today's lesson is "Live Within Your Limits." I wanted to make the lesson "Laugh at Your Limits," but was told by the team that no one feels like laughing after a day like you've just had.

Your exercise today is to begin making a list of the things you cannot do. Not impossible things like "Fly to the moon by flapping my arms," but things you have tried to do or dreamed of doing that you really can't do. In some cases it might be something you possibly could do if you abandoned everything else in your life or compromised your values, but it's something that you know is not your path.

Think back to your younger years and the things you wanted to be and do; things you now know will never happen. Think of some things you've been half planning to do but never gotten around to; things you should now delete and never think about again.

This is an especially difficult exercise because you have read and been told that you can do and be whatever you want. In other words, you've been lied to. What makes it a lie is not that you aren't capable of many different amazing things, because you are. That's the thesis of Release. But you are not capable of everything. Let that statement soak in: You are NOT capable of everything. Choosing to do one important thing means you will never accomplish several others.

This may sound, especially in the context of the frustrating day you've just had, quite negative and deflating. If you have an extreme ego, an overblown and artificial self image, it may well be a downer. But there is a very positive side to this truth, and it is this: Because you can't do everything you don't need to do everything..."

The words made me stop for a moment. I personalized the statement: Because I can't do everything, I don't need to do everything. I sensed a faint, but undeniable breeze of freedom course through my soul.

Because you can't do everything you don't need to do everything. Your unique package of limitations is a gift to free you from guilt for not doing everything, to free you from wasting energy by trying to do everything, to free you from the unrealistic demands of others who expect you to do everything. You cannot, therefore you don't even need to try! Decide today to live within your limits, to love your limits, and maybe in time, you will even be free to laugh at your limits.

This is the last phase of Harnessing Your History, the last stage in gathering the necessary raw material as fuel for the chain reaction. It began with Processing Your Pain, Embracing Your Encouragement, Admitting Your Abilities, and now, finally, choosing to Live Within Your Limits. If you have done these things thoroughly over the last several days, you are ready to fire the first neutron and begin the energy release that comes when you Focus Your Future!

It gets really good from here, believe me. Have a fine evening, a solid sleep, and prepare for the exciting next phase!

Love,
Len

I radioed the base and fought not to add a complaint to my check-in. Then I sat back and mulled over Len's letter. My anger at the futile hike slowly dissipated. It occurred to me that the frustration I felt at my inability to cross the river, as well as my irritation at the "wasted" time and energy from the hike, were the same emotions I felt when things didn't go as planned, either in business or in my personal life. In truth, the impossible river crossing hadn't frustrated and angered me, it had simply revealed a latent anger and frustration I lived with all the time. What was behind it? Today, a waypoint I couldn't reach by a self-imposed deadline, and then couldn't reach at all, had been the catalyst for those feelings. In my normal life back in civilization, other delayed or inaccessible "waypoints" prompted the same feelings to surface.

Why? Why was I frustrated in the midst of success? I'd succeeded in so many measurable ways, and yet I was still not satisfied. Over time, I'd developed a smoldering anger fed by the deep dissatisfaction at the core of my soul. I'd always believed that success in my own eyes and in the eyes of others would create peace and an unwavering sense of well being — but success hadn't delivered.

The impact of the day's frustrating activity, Len's words, and the new personal insights pounded at my heart. I felt an impending release. That evening as I wrote, the release came, with tears. I said goodbye to some dreams. I turned off the voices of people in my life, even a few from the past, who had tried to impose their dreams on me, or live their dreams through me. After I filled several pages, venting the frustration and anger, I smiled and uttered a deep sigh of relief, from far inside. I closed my eyes and again savored the words, "You don't need to do everything."

I fell asleep with a sense of emptiness I'd never experienced before: not the emptiness of despair, but the emptiness of anticipation — the emptiness of a hungry person about to sit down to a feast.

Day 8

For the second day in a row I woke up feeling good. I lay in bed for awhile wrestling with the suspicion that I was being set up again. I now knew how quickly a good feeling could be squelched. But in the end, Len's letter — and the fact that I was shifting from "harnessing my history" to "focusing my future" — made me trust my feelings, and crawl out of bed.

My clothes and footwear were completely dry, boosting my sense of well being. Scattered clouds drifted in the morning sky, but none of them looked like they would bring rain. I ate, entered the new destination in my GPS, and stepped outside.

The waypoint was southeast of me, which was unfortunate because I'd been hoping to walk on the trail heading south from the cabin. I decided to take it for a stretch anyway, since I did need to go south somewhat before cutting east.

There were a few rabbits and a pile of bear scat on the trail in my first fifteen minutes of walking. The latest bear sign didn't bother me as much as the first had. I was becoming convinced that most animals really were wary of people.

I followed the trail to the sharp bend west, as I had the day before. Since I was still a ways north of my destination, I decided to stay on the trail a bit longer. I was glad I did. Shortly after the westward bend I'd encountered the day before, the ground began dropping and the trail quickly switched back to the east. A short while later it jogged west, then back east again heading straight for my waypoint, still dropping.

After about an hour-and-a-half of walking I heard a faint roar and realized I must be getting close to the large, wild river. I got closer, the roar got louder, and then, just as I could see the ground dropping away to the river and mist rising, I saw the white waypoint box. I couldn't see a cabin, so I knew it wasn't my final destination for the day.

The paper in the box said:

Focus Your Future:
Define Your Destination

Imagine you live to the age of 85. Write three eulogies summarizing your life the way you would want a friend, a business colleague, and a family member to describe you.
Note: There is a nice place to sit by the falls. Take your time. The next camp is close by!

The camp's waypoint was printed at the bottom. I entered the numbers immediately and saw it was less than a mile away, likely on the trail further downstream. After taking a sip of water, I walked up a small path toward the roar. I realized I was at the very same waterfalls I'd been standing above the day before! I must have come within two hundred yards of this new waypoint.

When I looked down river, it was almost the same view I'd had yesterday, just a bit lower. A rustic, surprisingly comfortable bench made of poles was fastened between two trees, facing the falls. The canopy formed by the trees was so thick I was sure a person sitting on the bench would stay dry even in a downpour.

I sat down, took out my water, snacks, and journal. A cool air wafted off the water as I began to write. It was slow going. I realized that some comments which sounded positive from one of the imaginary eulogizers had negative implications for the other relationships. For instance, I wrote from the perspective of a friend, saying I was "always willing to drop everything and be there when needed, whether for fun or in a crisis." But as I thought about it, I realized that if I got married and had a family of my own, friendship would need to take a back seat to family. The same tensions arose in relation to work and family as well as work and friendship.

As I wrote, I found I could bypass those tensions by describing my 85-year-old dead self not merely in terms of what I did, but by who I was, in character. For instance, "loyal" or "humorous" worked no matter which relationship was on the front burner. I jotted down a little side note to think more about "being versus doing."

Despite the roar from the falls, I found the bench in the trees very conducive to this kind of thinking. Watching the water drop and looking out over the valley downstream made me think of the inevitable passage of time. Life felt short. I wanted to get home and flex the new inner muscles I was discovering and developing.

After an hour, I had a description of myself based on character qualities, not accomplishments. At one point I ran through the alphabet trying to find positive words I hoped would one day describe me — attentive, balanced, caring, dependable, entrepreneurial... I didn't know if that was the intention of the exercise, but I liked what I'd written. Thirty more minutes of scratching out words and adding new ones, and I had four pages of praise I would be proud to have read at my funeral.

With camp so close I decided to stay at the falls for lunch and walked a narrow path up toward my original lookout the day before, while chewing jerky and drinking vegetable juice. The mist shrouded me with a cool dampness, but I knew it would evaporate in the breeze and sun. Back at the bench I added a few more thoughts to the eulogies. Then, convinced I'd drained my creativity for this particular exercise, I moved down the trail toward camp.

The path paralleled the river, which no longer foamed, but was still moving quickly. The cabin was situated only a few yards back from the edge and was a clone of the others, except that this one had a window in the door covered by plywood. There were six toggles holding the wood in place. I turned them, and the plywood popped out, casting afternoon light into the small room.

I dumped my gear on the bed and left the door wide open while I found the outhouse. When I got back a squirrel was poking at my pack. It ran back away from the door and climbed the wall when I entered, so I backed out and walked a few yards away.

The squirrel quickly scooted out, realizing the cabin was not a safe place, and climbed into the low branches of the nearest tree where it sat chattering. I realized I'd made a mistake in leaving the door open, and was grateful it had not been a bear going after my pack.

"So, what do you think squirrel? If you live to be 85, what do you want people to say about you at your squirrel memorial?" I raised the pitch of my voice, stuck out my front teeth, and put on my best squirrel face. "'He could stuff his cheeks with the best of them.' 'His front teeth were always sharp.' 'He gave freely of his pinecones to less fortunate squirrels.' 'He was a proud, self-assured little rodent.'" I laughed at my own stupid humour, tossed a large pine cone at the squirrel which sent him scrambling into the higher branches, and then wandered into the cabin.

The cabin contained some supplies that had not been in the others: several one gallon water jugs; water purification tablets with instructions on how to use them; a reminder to refill my water bottles; a fishing rod and lures; a medium-sized cast iron frying pan; a bottle of cooking oil; and a long skinny filleting knife to clean fish. A bookshelf held some novels and assorted outdoor magazines, as well as a fishing guide.

I decided to lay down for a nap, but then remembered to radio in my safe arrival. I also realized I hadn't checked the white box. The instructions on the back of the box were simple:

Focus Your Future:
Define Your Destination

Harnessing Your History is gathering the raw material. It's time to fire the first neutron that begins the chain reaction and the energy release. This happens by Focusing Your Future.

Review your eulogies and underline anything you wrote that lines up with your current trajectory of life. That is, what things will eventually happen if you keep living the way you are now? Then circle the things you wrote that will not occur unless you make changes.

I scowled, knowing intuitively this would not be a particularly pleasant task, and brought my journal with me back to the bed. I did the underlining portion of the exercise, and as I'd expected, there was very little to underline. I rested my eyes for a while and then obediently worked my way through the circling. Achieving some of the circled items would simply require slight adjustments in my pattern of living, while others called for wholesale changes in my life. I took the assignment a bit further and wrote out the list of circled items, describing what would need to change for each to be fulfilled. When that was done, I rewarded my eyes with another rest that turned into a thirty-minute nap. I woke, rolled out of bed, and started to think about supper.

"Fresh fish would be nice," I thought. I flipped through the fishing guide and was glad to see that it illustrated how to clean a fish, something I'd never done before. My father was the fish cleaner in our home until he died.

I walked down to the river with the rod, and after a few tangled casts got the knack of tossing the hook nearly across the river. After a half dozen casts I was startled by a strike on the line, and in a few moments had a small flopping rainbow trout on the bank.

It took me longer to clean the fish than it had to catch it. When I was done it didn't look as neat and clean as when dad used to do it, but it was fresh and I was hungry. I excitedly fired up the burner, heated the oil, and got the fish frying. I also combined a mixture of powdered potatoes and dried vegetables in a pot, using most of my water to re-hydrate it. When the fish was done I put the pot on the burner to cook. I nibbled at the fish, but decided to wait and eat it with the potatoes. I filled the water jugs, added the tablets, and let them dissolve while I dug in.

I would've paid quite a few bucks for some butter or gravy for the potato/vegetable mixture, but it was still very good with the added fish. I washed it all down with tea and a little gorp, which I knew I should save for the trail, but I craved something sweet.

I put the frying pan outside on a stump and filled it with hot water to soak while I cleaned the pot and eating utensils. Then I made some tea and walked up and down the river bank enjoying the last hints of daylight.

My concern about not being able to sleep after taking two power naps proved unfounded. I couldn't even finish reviewing my notes from the previous day before my eyes involuntarily began to close. The gentle lapping of the river and the distant sounds of the falls were a lullaby clearing my mind, sedating me, until I was gone.

Day 9

I was desperately trying to impress the beautiful woman with an embellished account of my dangerous wilderness journey, but an irritating clunking sound kept interrupting my train of thought, forcing me to start my story over again and again. The noise had a slight metallic ring and I desperately wanted it to stop. But it persisted, got louder, and I woke suddenly with a pounding chest. What was that noise?

I walked quietly to the window and nearly stopped breathing when I saw a black bear trying to hold the frying pan in place with his paws while licking it rapidly. I'd left it dirty, outside — a cardinal sin in bear country. The pan was bouncing and banging while the bear licked and huffed, oblivious to my presence less than ten yards away. I didn't know what to do.

The bear was smaller than the ones I'd imagined stalking me at different times along the trail, and it didn't have the six inch fangs I'd pictured. Marsha's description of bear attacks on humans didn't seem to match the near comic performance I was watching. But I could tell, despite its thick glossy hair and teddy bear look, this was a muscular animal I did not want to tangle with.

It may have been the mix of fear and grogginess, tempered by inexperience and stupidity, I don't know, but without thinking I let out a loud "Hey!" The bear froze, glanced my way, and then sent dirt and leaves flying as its claws dug into the ground accelerating it away. In two or three seconds it was gone. I stood in silent amazement, both at my unthinking yell and at the power and speed displayed by the animal as it escaped. I wasn't sure if I should be more or less scared of bears than I had been. Clearly this bear, like most bears according to our training, was afraid of people. But equally clear was the fact that these

animals were deceptively strong and fast. If I came across one that wasn't afraid of me, I knew it would be no contest.

I carefully opened the door and stepped outside, then ran back to get my bear spray before retrieving the pan. It had not only been licked, but also chewed, bent, and punctured by some teeth, though not damaged beyond use. I washed it up before breakfast, still shaking my head and rolling my eyes at the carelessness of leaving it outside.

After breakfast I entered the new coordinates. The waypoint was only about two miles away. I figured I'd be there before midmorning, especially since the trail followed the river and looked like it was heading in the right direction. The wide, sloping path was easy walking. Sunlight wasn't yet hitting the valley bottom, so I wore my wool jacket to stave off the chill. I glanced back over my shoulder frequently to see if the bear was following for more easy food. Within twenty minutes I grew comfortable once again, though I did check the location of my bear spray at every corner.

The trail drifted from beside the river bank to a few hundred yards into the trees and then back to the river. At one point it crossed a creek bed with a very small trickle of water running toward the river, and when I checked my GPS I saw the waypoint was very close, fewer than one hundred yards away. The trail seemed to pass the waypoint, so I went straight toward it through the trees, angling away from the river.

I saw the white box at about thirty yards, fastened to a medium-sized spruce tree. When I got to it, I discovered that the small trickle was water from a creek that had been dammed by beavers, creating a large pond spreading far back into the forest. Lopsided, dead trees stood in the pool, drowned by the water. Three ducks took off splashing and squawking, and every few minutes a small trout broke the surface. I guessed that a large cone of mud and sticks in the middle of the water was the beaver lodge. There was wet mud pushed up near where I was standing, and it dawned on me that I was on the dam itself. It held the water level of the pond two or three yards higher than the trickle below, and ran for more than fifty yards in either direction. It was an impressive work of engineering.

The note in the box started out like the sign at a viewpoint on a nature trail. It briefly described the habits of beavers and pointed out that this particular dam was more than 100 years old. Successive generations of beavers had repaired it, added to it, and used it to provide safe habitat for themselves and a variety of other creatures. I looked at the small ridge running away from me in both directions, indicating the dam's maximum historical size. It penetrated into the woods much farther and higher than the water now rose. At one time the pond had been a small lake held in place by a much larger dam.

At the bottom of the page, just above the next coordinates, were a few simple words.

Dream.
If you could do anything at all
to leave your mark on this world,
what would it be?

Out of habit, I transcribed the words and coordinates into my journal, entered the numbers into my receiver, and then paused to think.

The question was not unlike ones I'd asked myself many times in the past. I had to admit though, that my "big-picture" questions often centered on getting or doing something that would be fun or pleasurable. Leaving a legacy, a positive mark after I was gone, was not an issue I'd concerned myself with. Even my involvement with various charities and community projects had more to do with networking and enjoying a good party than with a true concern for loftier issues.

I sat on a fallen tree the beavers had obviously chewed down recently — there were still green leaves on its branches — and began writing tentative answers to the question. Curing cancer or AIDS, ending poverty, creating world peace. My emotions were not engaged. While I believed that each of the ideas was good, I had no passion for any of them, perhaps because they seemed so huge, perhaps because there was nothing in my history or expertise to suggest I could contribute significantly to any of them. I laughed when I realized that my jottings could serve as generic notes for the speech portion of a beauty pageant.

I moved from dreaming to day-dreaming about the tasks waiting for me back home. I fiddled with my GPS and saw the next waypoint was four or five miles away. I told myself that I should probably get moving. I jotted down a few more things, packed up my journal, and was about to leave when an idea struck me. This beaver dam had been around for a hundred or more years. The beavers who first built it were long gone and yet there were beavers today — great, great grandkids of the original family perhaps — still keeping the dam functioning. I dug out my journal again and wrote under my list of possible dreams, "Whatever you do to leave your mark, make sure you enlist others to help, and instill in them the passion and ability to carry on after you're gone."

I felt some satisfaction with that new thought. Even though I hadn't identified a deep dream that resonated with me on an emotional level, I realized that even big, seemingly impossible dreams like ending a disease, poverty, or war felt more achievable when I saw them as multi-generational team efforts.

I walked out to the trail assuming that the next waypoint, hopefully the camp, would be on or near it. The trail continued to be extremely easy, giving me ample time for further dreaming. I thought of the eulogies I'd written, the idea of "being versus doing," and what I really wanted to do with my life. I'd already made enough money and had enough stuff to know that no amount would bring satisfaction. That was, in fact, part of why I was on this quest. My happiest moments were with close friends and family. My most fulfilling efforts were in the things which I saw made a positive and significant difference in the lives of others. A school trip I'd taken to Thailand with a relief organization twenty years earlier to work with orphans, remained the single most satisfying period of my entire life. What did that tell me?

The realization that, despite all my travels and education and earning and spending and playing in the past twenty years, nothing compared to that three-week service trip, made me stop and think. Whatever my deepest dream, and I was becoming aware that there *was* one buried deep in my heart, I knew it had to be about helping people somewhere, somehow. The religious workers I'd encountered on the relief trip made me think about the prayer exercise from Day 4, and I wondered where the hypothetical Creator might fit in with my dreams.

I took out my journal and recorded a few of those thoughts, then had a bite to eat before continuing down the trail. Two-and-a-half hours of casual walking after I left the beaver pond, I came around a corner and saw the cabin. To my left was the river I'd been following all day. Just beyond the cabin, and to the right, was another smaller river flowing into the first. I was sure it was the river I'd crossed on Day 6, so I zoomed out on the screen of my receiver and saw I was almost directly south of the Day 4/5 cabin on the ridge.

The new cabin sat in a small triangle of flat ground between the two rivers, surrounded by large pine trees. I saw two squirrels running and climbing, chasing each other around at a frantic speed. A sandbar ran out from the point of the triangle for another fifty yards before it disappeared into the merging rivers. It was the most beautiful camp so far, picture perfect, almost surreal. I realized I must be in the heart of the basin I'd seen from up on the ridge several days before. Since it was only 12:30, I looked forward to several more hours of daylight in this soul-calming place.

I went into the cabin, which was little different from the others. Hanging on the wall beside the white box was a painting of the campsite. It somehow captured the spirit of the place without attempting to reproduce every stick and stone in detail. The letters W-a-t were painted in a thin white script near the bottom right corner. I couldn't make out the rest of the name, as the painting had been scuffed. I wondered if the painter was someone who had taken the *Release* journey I was on.

When I opened the box, I realized the painting was placed very deliberately. The instructions said:

> *Focus Your Future:*
> *Picture Your Purpose*

As well as you can, write one crisp sentence defining your current understanding of your mission or purpose on this earth. (For an example, check the back of the painting.) Your answer to this question will integrate your deepest philosophical beliefs, your life situation, and everything you've learned through the Harnessing Your History phase of the adventure.

I copied out the words, as well as the next coordinates, and moved to the painting. Lifting it carefully off the wall, I turned it over and read the words handwritten on a fine piece of parchment glued to the back of the matting:

"The heavens declare the glory of God..."
My mission is to bring joy and peace by communicating the heart of God for his creation through my art.

Well, whoever it was, he or she certainly had it pinned. Creator or not, joy and peace were exactly what the painting communicated.

I wandered outside and into the sunshine on the sandbar where I noticed several different kinds of animal tracks — some made with hooves, some with paws, some the size of quarters, and some, which I assumed were bear, the size of my open hand. When I turned back I noticed a bench under a large tree facing the smaller river. This would have been a fine two- even three-night camp. I considered napping, but wasn't even remotely tired, so I grabbed my journal and went to the bench.

"A crisp sentence defining my understanding of my mission on earth," I said out loud to myself. "That's why I'm here. I was hoping you could tell me."

I flipped through my notes, rereading the portions I'd marked with little asterisks, because I felt they were especially important.

I wrote, "My mission is," and then leaned back closing my eyes, listening to the birds and lapping water, enjoying the gentle breeze. I added the words "to help," but then erased them and quickly wrote a phrase that surfaced in my imagination: "to alleviate the suffering of children." Something about it felt right for me. Now how was I going to do that? The painter achieved his or her mission via painting. How could I alleviate the suffering of children? I thought of the things I'd heard about and seen: child prostitution, slavery, illiteracy, children injured by landmines or born with AIDS, malnutrition, and, of course, orphans. After considering and discarding several possibilities, I settled on, "My mission is to alleviate the suffering of children by giving myself to a yet-to-be-determined cause, and mobilizing others to join me." I knew it needed to be more specific, and I knew I needed to research both the issues and the organizations that were already addressing them, but the phrase "alleviate the suffering of children" had captured my imagination. It was something for which I could get passionate. Based on the excited tension in my stomach, and the creative possibilities pushing their way to the front of my mind, I already was passionate about it.

I wondered about all the different life purposes that had been born in this spot. They were likely as diverse as the people who'd made the journey. Yet if every one struck a chord in someone's heart the way this half-baked idea had in mine, the world was certainly a better place, simply because the question of purpose had been asked. I wished there was a log book in the cabin where the fruits of that question could be recorded and read by future travelers. I made a note to suggest it to Len.

Eventually, I did lay down for a while. Then I began slowly making supper and boiling water in a large pot, which a sign on the table suggested I do to replenish my drinking water. I radioed in and ate a bland but filling meal of what may have been a tasty pasta dish prior to dehydrating.

There was no fishing rod, another observation to pass on to Len. Another trout would've been nice. I used the remaining daylight hours to explore along the river banks, skip stones, and write down new thoughts that came to my mind. I wished for my laptop and an internet connection to begin exploring options for my mission.

When it grew dark I lay on my bed for some time, just listening. I heard an owl calling through the trees, and a distant yapping that must have been coyotes. There was the occasional splash of fish in the rivers. Eventually all the sounds seemed to merge with my breathing, and I fell into a very deep, dreamless sleep.

Day 10

Seven days had passed since my last contact with people. I couldn't remember seven *hours* alone apart from sleep prior to this trip. I missed human contact, mostly my girlfriend's, only at rare moments through the day, and realized I was becoming comfortable with solitude.

After a quick breakfast, I refilled my water bottles and drank a belly full from the pot of water I'd boiled the night before. It tasted awful, but was at least, theoretically, bacteria free.

The new waypoint was southeast of my current location, which meant I had to cross the smaller of the two rivers. I didn't feel like getting wet at the start of my day, especially since the sky was overcast. I began to walk north along the bank where there was a good trail, hoping to find a crossing. Fewer than 200 yards upstream was a rough bridge of three squared logs lying side by side. A heavy yellow rope about three feet above the logs was tied between trees on opposite banks to provide a handhold for balance. I crossed easily and turned left, downstream, following first the small creek and then the larger combined river. The trail was an extension of the one I'd been on the day before, so travel continued to be easy. A grouse and two rabbits added to the scenery, and I saw a deer cross the trail with a bound and disappear into the trees.

The waypoint was only two miles away, give or take, so I doubted it would be the next camp. The trail brought me to within fifty yards of the destination indicated on the screen, at which point I turned right, off the trail, and immediately noticed a rock outcropping through the trees. The white box was fastened to a tree near the base of the disintegrating rock, which ran several hundred feet away from the trail. It looked to me as though the rock had been disturbed, turned over, and broken up, both by nature and people. The area appeared to be a small quarry of some kind.

When I opened the box, the first thing I saw was a blue-handled rock pick leaning against one side, and some safety goggles. There were also a few chunks of rock — some yellowish stones that looked pretty plain on the outside, but that had been broken open to reveal bands of color. There was also another one of those scary sealed envelopes. I took the pick out to read the note on the back of the box.

> *Find four of these agates.*
> *Break one or two open until you know what they look like. Keep two intact for cutting and polishing. Then open the envelope.*

I drank some water and walked over to the outcrop. I found one roundish stone about two inches in diameter, put on the goggles, placed it on a boulder, and smashed it with the pick. It split into hundreds of little pieces and revealed nothing but plain rock inside. I went back to the box and looked carefully at the outer surface of the samples. I noticed they were a little bumpier than a rounded stream-bed stone, even slightly pitted. They seemed to be coated with a layer of cement that only thinly concealed the richer mineral underneath. I dug around a bit, rolling some larger rocks and slabs out of the way before I saw a suspicious stone lying in the mix. It was heavier than it looked, and I was so sure it was an agate that I was reluctant to break it open. But I did, with some difficulty, and sure enough the plain outer surface gave way to reveal bands of color.

I moved more rubble around and found what I was sure were several more agates, two of which already had some of the outer surface chipped away revealing the waxy looking inner layers. I smashed one open just to be sure, and then selected four to take with me. The entire exercise took less than an hour. The sealed envelope revealed a lengthy debrief and application:

Master Your Moment!
Gather Your Goals

You've looked back to Harness your History. You've looked ahead to Focus Your Future. Now it is time to Master Your Moment!

You're probably familiar with the Latin phrase "carpe diem" — seize the day. Originally, the phrase meant to seize the pleasures of the moment without concern for the future. That is NOT what we mean here. The future is important. By Master your Moment we mean "make

105

every moment of your life count by taking responsibility for the opportunities placed before you, and for the dreams planted in you."

In our metaphor, if Harnessing Your History is gathering up the raw materials, and Focusing Your Future is firing the initial neutron, Mastering Your Moment is the utilization of that energy release. The first step in doing this is to Gather Your Goals. Goals turn your dreams into reality.

Here is your assignment: Never forgetting about your history, your dreams, or your purpose as you currently understand them, formulate three to five Life Goals. These are goals, which if achieved, will make your life a true success. Then, based on those life goals, come up with three to five ten-year goals, three to five annual goals, and finally three to five goals for the next three months.

The quarterly goals are very important. They make the difference between capturing time and simply putting in time. Your life purpose may look overwhelming, your life goals impossible, and your ten-year goals too burdensome. But when you identify a few things you can do in the next three months, that's a bite-sized chunk. And every time you see progress, even incremental, toward the things that really matter, there is an energy release and the chain reaction continues. Progress releases energy. And here's a tip: You can accomplish far less in a year than you think, and far more in a decade than you can imagine.

Each of the agates you have represents one layer of goals. Just as you've been digging, gathering, and hammering to find the gemstones, it's time to "hammer out" your goals.

And, as the months, years, and decades pass, be sure to rework each layer.

It's very easy to waste your life: many people do. If you waste enough hours you waste a day, if you waste enough days you waste a year, and if you waste enough years you will waste your life. There is only one way to avoid this common fate: Master Your Moment. Fully utilize today and tomorrow and every day that you draw breath. Use your minutes and hours in ways that move you toward where you want to be one year, fifty years, even one thousand years from now.

"Quite a lecture, Len," I said out loud.

Goals. This was starting to sound like work. But I realized as I reread the note, that none of the goal setting I'd done in my life had been anchored in the larger context in which I now found myself. Most of my goal setting had been weekly, with the odd yearly goal showing up as a New Year's resolution at the end of December or beginning of January. I'd never wrestled with anything as all-encompassing as lifetime goals. I quickly saw how the ten-year, annual, and quarterly goals would flow naturally from a sense of purpose and long-term direction, and how they would create a cumulative sense of progress.

I dutifully transcribed the full text of the letter into my journal, along with the new coordinates. I entered the waypoint in my GPS and continued down the trail, contemplating some lifetime goals. One that rose up quickly was to find my "sweet spot" by the age of fifty, hopefully earlier, and live there for the remainder of my days. I defined "sweet spot" as the place where my work, service activities, and relationships all fit me like a glove, where they synced fully with my philosophy of life, my passions and abilities, and, of course, my still-preliminary life mission.

A light drizzle began to fall, so I stopped and put on my tattered rain gear. I entertained several more hypothetical life goals, and by the time my stomach told me it was past lunch, I had a tentative list of four.

As I ate, I reflected on the seeming speed with which I was crystallizing some of the big issues of my life. I'd always viewed self analysis and goal setting as an unwieldy and lengthy process too huge to tackle. But now, spurred on by the solitude and the loaded questions at each waypoint, along with the related daily activity, my brain and heart seemed to be firing on all cylinders. The fresh air and rugged beauty certainly didn't hurt, and the bottom line was that I'd done more introspection and personal planning in a few days than I'd managed in all my previous years.

The cabin appeared at mid-afternoon. It had been the longest, though not the most difficult, hike of the week. By my estimate I'd walked at least nine miles.

The site was nothing special, but only in contrast to the last two. Prior to the trip I would have been awed by the location. The river still flowed by, large trees branched out and up toward the wet sky, and for now at least, it was home. I radioed in and then removed the plywood window covering in the door. It was still drizzling, so I worked on my ten-year and annual goals inside, with the cabin door wide open for light. I decided to leave the quarterly goals till after supper.

Following a nap, I cooked up another nondescript "high-energy balanced meal" and washed it down with some apple juice.

Then I set to work on my three-month goals. I didn't want to rush this stage, since I knew these goals would impact my schedule immediately upon arriving home. I also knew they needed to align with my annual, decadal, and life goals. One of my new goals was to gather material and become somewhat of an expert on global children's issues. Another related to some relationships I wanted to rekindle, and the third expressed something which had not even been on my radar screen prior to the journey. It simply said, "Check out the God thing."

I tweaked and fiddled with the wording of my goals by lamplight for a few hours after supper, shivering in the wet chill. Then I stripped down, put on some clean, dry long underwear, and crawled into my sleeping bag. A light rain hissed on the roof and ground, creating a white noise that ushered me into the world of my imagination.

Day 11

Somewhere in the night it dawned on me that I still didn't know exactly how long the journey would last. I woke up with the question rolling through my brain. "Allow for three weeks" the registration had said, and Len had simply reiterated those words on the evening of Day 2 in response to Shane's question. I might have one night left, but I might have seven or eight!

On one level, I was content to stay out for another seven days or seven weeks, but as I prepared breakfast (I will never eat powdered eggs again as long as I live!) I realized my food supply was getting low — there were perhaps three days left. Either I had another cache coming up, or I would finish in just a few more days. I reasoned that since I was on the last major segment, *Master Your Moment*, the end was nearer rather than farther.

I knew as soon as I started walking that I was going to lose the pleasant trail I'd been on for three days. The river and trail veered away to the left, changing direction from southwest to south, but my waypoint required I stay on a generally southwest course. The base camp was quite a distance to the west, so I knew if I only had a few days left they could be long ones. The broken clouds and moderate breeze made conditions ideal for hiking.

As I moved away from the river, there was no clear path other than the game trails that seemed to appear and disappear randomly. I was able to walk on some of them for a few hundred yards at a time, but then they would turn away from my bearing. However, apart from one swampy patch of red willows that I could've used a machete to hack my way through, the walking was fairly easy. The ground sloped steadily upward and the pine trees were large and well spaced with little underbrush.

A motion down to the left caught my eye, and I saw a red fox slinking away, looking over its shoulder in my direction. In the first hour, several grouse had flushed off the ground into the trees, following me with their eyes as I moved by. No wonder a fox was hunting in the neighborhood.

After about three-and-a-half miles, the ground began to slope downward slowly. My waypoint was getting close. After another mile the ground seemed to drop away. Below me the sand petered out, exposing bedrock, and a spectacular little canyon snaked its way through the rock. Some of the S curves had cut through, creating stone pillars with water running on both sides. It was a spectacular sight. I dug out my camera and took several shots, then looked around and saw the white box on a tree. Before I got to the box, I noticed a rope bridge I hadn't seen earlier, crossing the canyon.

I ran down the slope, ignoring the warnings I'd gotten in training, and went right by the box to look at the bridge. There were three main ropes — one for the feet and one on each side for the hands. Every sixteen inches or so there was a rope from each of the sides down to the lower, thicker foot rope. The little squares of open air between the ropes were strung with heavy netting. It looked impossible to fall off the bridge, but I didn't like what I saw — I wasn't much for heights. After glancing up and down the canyon for alternatives, I grudgingly accepted that it would have to do.

I took my pack off and walked back up to the box. Inside was the next waypoint and another set of instructions.

Master Your Moment:
Form Strategic Habits

Goals are the dreams of life; but habits are the stuff of life. The only way you will achieve your goals is by forming habits that move you toward them. Just as the water flowing below you has been running for millennia, slowly carving its path through the rock, your habits are the things which will ultimately determine the outcome of your life, for good or ill. Time will pass no matter what you do; where you apply yourself habitually determines the pattern you will carve — the mark you will leave.

Look back at your yearly, decadal, and life goals, and describe the daily, weekly, monthly, and yearly habits that will be required for you to reach those goals. If you do not establish strategic supporting habits, nothing will happen. This is where most goal setters fail. I repeat: If you do not establish strategic supporting habits, nothing will happen. However, if you formulate the right habits, progress toward your goals is inevitable. Your habits and routines predict and determine the final outcome of your life — the ultimate result of your energy release.

The truth of what I'd just read made me stop and think for a few minutes before I copied it out. Who would think that water could cut rock? But it does, through the combination of natural persistence and time. I thought of the Grand Canyon, a much larger version of what I was gazing down upon now.

"If water can do that to rock," I thought, "a habit could lead me to a completely different place in ten or twenty or fifty years."

I liked the word "inevitable." So much in my life that I still hoped to do could indeed happen, if I stopped hoping and simply engaged the necessary habits.

I decided to endure the bridge crossing before I spent time grappling with the habits exercise. The span was only about fifteen yards but the depth of the canyon looked to be more than one hundred feet. The ropes swayed with every step. Just before I got across, a clip on my pack caught the net and almost made me lose my balance. When I finally reached solid footing I was breathing hard and my heart was pumping like I'd just done a workout.

I walked a few yards up the slope to the right where there was a flat place to sit and think. It gave me a good view of the canyon and I thought I could see a space in the trees where the larger river ran away to the south.

I took out my journal, drank some water, had a snack, and began to make my list. The concept of yearly habits intrigued me. I'd always assumed a habit would have a much greater frequency than yearly. What did I need to do yearly to reach my goals? It occurred to me that a retreat of some kind where I could do regular self examination and make course corrections would be a very beneficial annual habit. A monthly habit I settled on had to do with reviewing my finances and tweaking investments. I decided I would do something weekly to explore my spirituality, whether it was to read a book, attend a place of worship, or spend time on an internet discussion forum.

I had a hard time coming up with daily habits. I didn't even exercise daily. Finally I landed on making sure I did a short inspirational reading of some kind, and communicated with a close friend either on the phone, in person, or by email. When I was done, I had two daily habits, four weekly, two monthly, and three annual. At first it didn't seem like much, but I realized that if I kept these habits, progress toward my goals was indeed "inevitable."

I sat for at least twenty minutes after I was done writing, enjoying the view and trying to absorb the sun whenever it poked through the scattered clouds. I entered the coordinates in my receiver and saw that the next waypoint was only a mile to the west. I reviewed my notes from previous days and counted nearly eighty pages, though some had a lot of white space since I started each day on a clean page.

Eventually I got up, stretched, yelled to see if there was an echo (there wasn't), put on my pack, and started walking. I was surprised to discover a footpath headed in the right direction. Sure enough, in a little more than half-an-hour I came to the cabin.

At first I couldn't figure out why the cabin was situated where it was. The trees were small, and there was no view or any other redeeming factor.

I laughed and said, "You're getting spoiled!" Two weeks ago a place like this would have seemed like heaven.

I noticed a well just beyond the cabin. It was the classic round rock wall I always thought of when I heard the word "well," even though I'd never seen one before. It didn't have the bucket on a rope dangling from a beam with a hand crank, but when I got close I saw water running freely out of a hole in one side. There was a small wooden sign that said "Drink up! The water is pure and cold!" I quickly obeyed and then dumped out the remaining boiled water and refilled my bottles.

My stomach growled and I looked at my watch. It was already 2:00 pm! I decided to eat a larger meal right away and have a lighter lunch before bed. There wasn't much to choose from. I drank my last box of vegetable juice while I cooked up a colorful dehydrated meal labeled "chicken dinner." The colors seemed to be chunks of dried carrots, peas, corn, and an orange substance that I guessed might be yams. I added a little salt, and it went down quite well with some tea made from the cold spring water.

The white box in the cabin contained nothing except my next coordinates. I was disappointed. It was still early and there wasn't much to look at in the new location. Another lecture from Len with an additional exercise would have been welcome. I called in and had to fight to keep from asking how the others were doing and how many more days I had. I missed my girlfriend more than ever and thought that if she were present

I'd propose to her on the spot. I decided to accelerate the ring shopping when I got home.

I unpacked and repacked all my gear. There was definitely less than three days' food left. I took out my agates and tried to scrape off the outer layer of rock. I entered the next waypoint and went for a walk with my GPS and bear spray. The footpath curved off to the south as the river had, while my waypoint was to the northwest. There was a lot of underbrush among these smaller trees, and I didn't look forward to a traverse through it the next morning. But I did notice with some joy that my new line of travel was almost a straight line toward the base.

I went inside and noticed a thick book on the corner shelf, *The Complete Works of Jack London*. I lit the lamp and read a story about sled dogs and another one about starting fires in the winter. I dozed off, got up and had my snack, then read some more. My eyes eventually got heavy, so I turned off the lamp and fell asleep thinking about what it would be like to do my trip in the winter with a dog team.

Day 12

I slept well and woke refreshed. It was threatening to become a pleasant pattern. I wrote out a list of reasons why I thought I was sleeping so well. Some were obvious — exercise and fresh air — but when I thought about it more, I realized I was experiencing a sense of peace rarely felt in my regular rush. I also noted an increased clarity about the big issues of life, and the anticipation of what lay ahead, as contributing factors to my new ability to rest deeply.

I did an "eeny-meeny-miny-mo" with my two remaining breakfast pouches, and ended up with oatmeal and banana chips. The oatmeal had the usual raisins and milk powder mixed in, but also dried cranberries, giving it some extra zest. A bonus of the decreasing rations was that my pack was becoming light. Based on the remaining food and the direction of travel, it looked like I had maybe another two days, before reaching the base.

The wind was lighter and the sky was packed more tightly with clouds than the day before, but there were still strips of blue. It neither looked nor felt like rain, but I was no forecaster, so I couldn't say for sure.

I fired up the GPS to get my line of travel. So far I hadn't needed the spare batteries, and an icon showed the originals still held 50 percent of their power. I started walking, made sure I was going in the right direction, and turned it off. The waypoint looked about five miles away, so I was sure it would be a challenging day unless I found a trail.

Within minutes I could tell I was climbing. One hour along and the trees began thinning. At times I could see quite a distance ahead, and the slope always continued. There were many obstacles to work my way around — fallen trees, boulders, and tiny five or ten-foot cliffs. The slope was not extreme, but it was steady, and I was sweating hard when I stopped for my first water break. I was surprised by how little horizontal distance the GPS showed I'd covered. Somewhere near the end of the second hour I had to navigate down into, through, and up out of a steep, dry gully. This took another full hour. The breeze grew stiff and the last bits of blue were obscured by fast-moving clouds.

In the fourth hour I realized the ground sloped away both to my right and left, while straight ahead it rose more steeply. I was on a ridge, the side of a mountain, and I was actually tiring — not as much as on Day 6 — but I was feeling it in my legs and lungs. When there was still a mile to go to the waypoint I was so hungry I decided to stop for lunch. Sitting still got me chilled. I put on my wool jacket and attempted to doze, but every time I was on the brink of sleep, thoughts of bears made me open my eyes and look around.

My legs and back felt stiff as I got going again, and I wondered if I'd been drinking enough water. I laughed at the thought of someone who was eating so much dehydrated food becoming dehydrated.

"You're losing it," I said out loud.

The last mile took more than an hour. It was steep, I was tired, and downed trees interspersed with boulders forced me into a wandering course. Suddenly, I found myself above the tree line with a spectacular panoramic view. In front of me, the rock rose for several hundred more yards, blocking out the view to the northwest. In every other direction I could see for miles. I was sure I could make out the ridge where I'd stayed on nights four and five, the deep valley with the creek I'd crossed on Day 6, as well as the river I'd followed on days eight, nine, and ten. A compressed summary of my hike and the lessons I'd learned raced through my mind as I scanned the scene. The rugged beauty seemed to stream through my senses straight to my soul, speaking to me nonverbally, pouring life into my spirit. I wondered: Was nature speaking to me? Or was it a Creator? The Creator? For several minutes I pondered what, if any, difference it would make to me if this beauty was a deliberate creation rather than coincidence.

The waypoint was off to my right. I went down off the ridge into the scattered trees and began working my way around the side of the mountain. Just back from a small landslide area, I saw the cabin. It looked completely out of place, stuck up where no one except the owners of an adventure camp would ever build. But then I saw a pile of rotting logs indicating the remains of another much older structure, and just beyond the ruins there was a hole in the side of the hill indicating a mine. I dropped my pack at the door of the new cabin, went over to the

121

hole, and walked in slowly. Unlike the mine on Day 5, this one went in for about fifteen feet, dropped straight down for eight more, and then sloped about 45 degrees down in the direction of the peak. Below the hole in the ground were the tailings of the mine spreading out like a fan through the scattered trees. I couldn't believe how much rock had come out of the hole.

I went over to the newer cabin and straight to the box to see my lesson for the day. I felt mentally starved by the large gap since finishing my habit list the day before, and was eager to keep moving forward.

The first thing I saw was a chocolate bar, which I immediately devoured. The box also contained a laminated piece of paper with an old photograph and several paragraphs in a small font below it. Above the picture, in dark felt pen, were written the words, *Read This First.* It was leaning against the back of the box, concealing the laminated paper with the new coordinates and some further instructions.

I took out the first piece of paper and saw that the picture was of a man standing in front of a mine on the side of a mountain. The date "1901" was written on the bottom of the picture. I immediately recognized the mountain in the picture as the one I was on. In fact, unless I was mistaken, the mine was the one I'd just peaked into. I went outside and compared the picture with the mountainside. Sure enough, I was able to put myself in a place just down from the mine that gave me a nearly identical view of the slope, minus the old miner. There were some trees on the slope above the mine in the picture that weren't there now, and some existing ones that weren't in the picture, but it was amazing how little had changed in more than a hundred years.

I sat down on a boulder and read the dense print below the picture:

David Singer made a fortune gold mining in Nevada in the mid-1800s. Then he lost it all in a business venture in San Francisco. He headed north looking for more gold and found himself here.

Mr. Singer prospected the valley to the northeast and staked a claim on this mountainside, convinced there was a large vein of gold in the bedrock. He was unable to find financial backing and couldn't afford to hire anyone, so in 1889 he began digging by himself. He tunneled 150 feet under the slide area you see. Then he dug another 175 feet through blue clay. But that was just the start. He kept going — a further 400 feet through a mix of clay, coarse gravel, and boulders. At that point he hit bedrock and began doing shafts and drifts up and down the surface of the bedrock looking for his vein of gold.

For 12 years he persevered in his dream, hauling every bit of loosened ground all the way back to the surface. But then he ran out of money and credit, his arthritis hampered his mobility, and he was forced to quit. He moved to a nearby town where he tried, until his death in 1914, to convince investors to hire workers to expose the vein of gold he was so sure existed. But while there has been plenty of gold found in the surrounding valleys, none has been found on this entire mountain, even with modern equipment. There is no gold here.

Note: It is safe to go into the mine for the first 50 feet. Beyond that the timber shoring is too rotten to trust.

"Thanks, but no thanks," I said. "I've already gone far enough."

The story of Mr. Singer was fascinating, but tragic. Maybe he'd just gotten lucky in Nevada and really didn't know much about mining. But no one could argue that he wasn't a hard worker — the tons of rock he'd dumped out of the hole proved he was. He had great faith and passion, even if they weren't based in reality.

I wandered back into the cabin, wondering what the application might be. It was quite dark inside, so I pulled out my flashlight to read the other note from the back of the box.

Master Your Moment:
Stop Spinning!

Most people do things which make absolutely no sense based on the facts, like spinning their tires as fast as possible, trying to gain traction on an icy road. David Singer dug for twelve years where there was no gold, while men in the valleys and on the other slopes around him were making a living; some were even getting rich. A dream is not enough... passion is not enough. We must also contend with reality.

Do you have any dead ends in your life? Is there a job, a relationship, a spending pattern, an activity that costs you several hours each week but doesn't contribute to the destination you seek? Are there dreams that should die, goals that should be revised, habits that must end? Are you taking the easy route in some areas, trading the dreams of a lifetime for the pleasures of the moment? Begin to narrow your focus, eliminate your 'want to's'— the things you want to do in the short term — and create space for your 'have to's,' the things you must do to achieve your dreams and accomplish your mission.

Your assignment is to create a "stop-doing" list of at least 25 things you will stop today, for the sake of your dreams and goals. This exercise is one aspect of the larger issue of simplicity, which we hope you are learning to value during the sparse lifestyle of this journey. Often, the focusing of your future leads to greater simplicity in your life, but we find that people need a little extra push to stop expending emotional energy on things which make no sense at all. Be ruthless!

On the side of a mountain, next to David Singer's useless twelve-year hole in the ground, those words had impact. By the time I got the lantern lit and sat down with my journal, I already had a handful of things for my "stop-doing" list. It wasn't hard to say goodbye to my fantasies of becoming an Olympic middle-distance runner. Most such athletes were retired by my age, but I spent an inordinate amount of time daydreaming about the impossible possibility, spinning my tires. Some other obvious little habits needed to go, and my TV time and aimless internet use needed severe curtailing.

There were also deeper, more difficult issues I needed to wade through. I recognized some grudges I carried that took far too much mental energy to sustain. I somehow needed to drop that load. In a flash of self awareness, I saw myself daily ridiculing people who held to social and political views different from mine. That habit also needed to cease. Each time I added something to my list, an increasing sense of freedom took hold.

When I was done my list of nearly three dozen items, I became aware of a rising energy at my core. I felt like everything had finally come together. I even wrote in my journal "I'm done! I could go home right now!" I knew then that I would be at the base camp the next day.

I laid out my food to see exactly what was left. Instead of making another "gourmet dinner," I combined bits and pieces of remaining snacks and lunches and ate the things I liked. I saved a small baggie of dried fruit and nuts for the trail the next day. In an emergency I could always cook up the last dinner.

I went outside and radioed the base. The reception was choppy, perhaps because the mountain was between me and the base. Feeling excited about the end of the hike I added, "See you tomorrow!" to my call. Andrea laughed but said nothing more. I poked around outside as the valley beneath me darkened. It was chilly enough to see my breath, so I went back inside and did a thorough review of my notes by lamplight. I thought of a few more things to stop doing, and then crawled stiffly into bed for my last sleep alone in the wilderness.

Day 13

I woke once during the night to the sound of wind and rain, groaned, rolled over, and went back to sleep. When I woke just after 7:00 am, the rain was gone and a shaft of sunlight painted the wall beside me. My legs were tight, but not as stiff as I'd worried they might be.

I cooked and ate my last instant breakfast with a flourish. After eating I went outside and took some pictures. The light was perfect, shining directly on the cabin, the mine, and the peak above me. I entered the coordinates and saw my destination was nearly a mile short of the base camp. I doubted there was an out camp so close to the end, and hoped it was an intermediate waypoint of some kind. It looked like a fair jaunt, but I was quite sure the base was my ultimate destination for the day. There was going to be real food for dinner!

I wasn't sure whether to continue around the mountain in the counter clockwise direction I'd taken to get to the cabin, or if I should get back on the south side. From what I recalled, it was easier walking on the south where I'd been yesterday, but doing the south side would require some of that despised backtracking and going up onto the ridge before making any forward progress. I decided to gamble and keep going along the north side of the ridge.

The wind was stiff, so I put on a nylon shell I hadn't yet used. I walked by the mine, marveling again at the effort David Singer had poured into that hole. Then I angled slightly upward as I worked around the mountain, hoping the height would give me a better idea which way to go when I cleared the peak.

An hour later I found myself on the northwest side looking down on a slope that seemed to go on forever. The bedrock turned into a slide that flowed into shrubs, small trees, and, finally, heavy timber. The timber stretched downward for what looked like five more miles before the ground rose again to the next peak. I yodeled, or rather tried to yodel, but the wind swept away my effort without an echo.

"Somewhere out there is my dinner!" I said.

I checked the receiver for my direction of travel before walking quickly down toward the timber. Several large brown shapes suddenly appeared and began moving into the trees. I frantically dug out my binoculars and saw that they were elk, the first ones I'd ever seen in the wild! They must have been bedded down in the brush and been woken and spooked, understandably, by my yodeling. As suddenly as they'd appeared, they were gone.

I was still two or three hundred yards above the forest when I saw two large trees stripped of branches about eight feet up, wrapped with several fluttering pieces of flagging tape. Then I noticed a line of flagging tied to brush extending in both directions up the slope away from the two large trees. It was like a funnel directing trekkers to what I was sure must be a trail.

I was right. And it was a beautiful trail, the best yet. There were slight ruts from ATVs, and the faint footprints of previous hikers. It was a wide, well-traveled downhill trail — easy going compared to my entire day of uphill hiking the day before.

I made good time, sipping on water as I walked, stopping only once for a snack. Three deer, a doe and two fawns, were standing together in the middle of the trail as I rounded one corner. They stared at me for a few seconds before bounding off, their white tails waving goodbye. The thick timber sheltered me from the wind, and I grew quite warm even with the easy walking.

It still wasn't lunch time when I neared the waypoint. With about two hundred yards to go, another wide trail came in from the right, and a few yards further one came in from the left. I felt like I was on edge of civilization.

I was craning my neck looking for the waypoint marker when I heard a yell from behind me. I quickly turned and was surprised to see Shane jogging toward me, gear bouncing, with a big smile on his face.

"Am I glad to see you!" he said excitedly.

"Likewise!" I replied. We shook hands and immediately started comparing our experiences, but then agreed we should get to the waypoint first.

Shane saw it before I did — a white waypoint box twenty feet up in the air, suspended on a cable between two trees. Beside the box and fastened to the same cable was a large pulley. A heavy rope went through the pulley. On the ground at one end of the rope was a climbing harness, and at the other end, a four-foot metal bar.

"What's the deal with that?" Shane asked.

"I think someone is supposed to get pulled up to the box," I said.

"How can we do that? It's not a block and tackle to give us mechanical advantage. Neither one of us is big enough to lift the other."

"No," I said, "But if Jennifer came along we could pull her up."

"Yeah, I bet you're right. I wonder how long she'll be?"

"Hard to say. I guess it depends what time she got up and how far she's coming."

We decided to eat lunch and wait for Jennifer. It was a lot of fun sharing our stories. I told Shane about the bear I'd seen. It turned out he'd seen three, all while hiking. One had been on a trail and taken off as soon as he saw it. The others were together on a ridge high above him. We talked for more than half-an-hour and were just beginning to share some of our lessons when we saw Jennifer coming down the trail.

When she saw us she waved, and as she got close I saw that she had a black eye and a cut on her cheek.

"What happened to you?" I asked.

"What do you mean?" she said.

"You've got a trophy shiner and a cut on your cheek," Shane said.

"Oh yeah, that was two days ago. I was stepping over a wet log and my foot slipped. Next thing I know my face bounces off the log and I'm sitting in the dirt. How bad does it look?"

"Oh it's nothing a little cosmetic surgery won't fix," Shane said. Jennifer laughed, punched him in the arm, and then insisted that we have a group hug.

"What's the story here?" she said looking up at the box and the rope.

We explained our theory to her and she quickly shed her pack and jacket and slipped into the harness. It had to be adjusted down for her slight build.

"Don't drop me!" she ordered as we began to walk slowly away pushing the metal bar with our hands and stomachs. She rose easily, and in less than a minute was on the ground with the envelope in her hands. We tore it open and read:

Master Your Moment:
Pick Your Partners

Life is meant to be lived in community. You need to take responsibility for your own values and decisions and direction, but once your course is set, you need help to keep the habits required to reach your goals and realize your dreams.

Before you leave for home, be sure to make a list of people you know who can help you solidify the things you've learned and decided, and encourage you along the journey. Look for at least one mentor for each key area in which you now know you need to grow. Make contact with them soon and take responsibility to meet with them regularly. Some of these partners will be older, wiser, or at least well ahead of you in your growth areas. Others will be peers. You need both. And when you see the benefit of such mentoring, I hope you will decide to pass on your growing wisdom to others as well.

We will supply an alumni list that you can check for former adventurers who live near you. In addition, we encourage you to meet at least once in the next year with the others who journeyed with you.

Follow the trail down to the base. You're almost done!

Jennifer let out a whoop and Shane and I joined her. We each copied out the assignment in our log books. Then laughing and talking, we walked the final distance to the base.

Len was sitting on the deck drinking coffee when we came into the clearing at the camp. He quickly rose and strode out to meet us with a handshake and a hug.

"Congratulations!" he said. You made it." Then seeing Jennifer he commented, "Ouch! Looks like you did a face plant."

Jennifer explained her mishap and Len said, "Well after you get cleaned up we'll have Randy take a look at you. But I think you'll survive."

"The next thing on the agenda is dinner at 5:00, so you have lots of time to get cleaned up. You might want to do the partner exercise from the last waypoint while it's still fresh in your minds."

We talked for a few more minutes and then noticed three hikers coming into the clearing from the trail we'd just been on. It was Jonathon, Marsha, and Randy.

"Hey, it looks like you guys have been out for a walk, too," said Shane. They all just smiled a funny kind of smile and looked at Len.

Len explained, "They were on the same hikes you three just did."

"What?!?" we all said in unison.

"We are your guardian angels," said Randy theatrically, throwing back his shoulders and putting his arms out like wings.

"Let me get this straight," I said. "You were following us?"

Marsha nodded and said, "Yep, I followed you, Randy followed Jennifer, and Jon followed Shane."

"How close were you following us?" Jennifer asked suspiciously.

"We were never within sight of you," Randy said looking at the other two, who nodded. "We have all the waypoints in our receivers and each of your packs has a location transmitter in the frame. If you didn't radio the base one day, or if the transmitter indicated you weren't moving for a long time, we'd come running. It's just a safety precaution."

"And it's also an important lesson," Len added, putting on his teaching voice. "There are many times in life when you'll feel like you're all alone, that no one knows what you're going through, and no one cares. It's not true. You are never really alone on your journey. Sometimes it takes some searching and observing to find them, but there are almost always people who care for you. In fact, we're here for you for life. And in the absence of people, you still have a Creator who made you for a purpose. You're never alone on the journey." He paused and then reminded us, "Dinner at five!"

I thanked my "guardian angel" and then headed for my room. I wrote out Len's words "you're never alone on the journey" before I did anything else. Then I had a long shower, scrubbing myself from head to toe. It felt great.

I changed into a sweat suit I'd left with my gear at the lodge, and sat down on the overstuffed chair in my room to think and write some more. Just before 5:00 pm I walked down to the dining room and took a seat. The others soon followed.

When everyone was settled, Len proposed a toast to the three of us, and then the feast began. Soup, salad, roast beef, fish, mashed potatoes, mixed vegetables, and three dessert options. I stuffed myself. As we ate dessert we were each given the opportunity to stand and share a significant lesson from the week. Our lessons were completely unique, but all powerful and profound.

Jennifer shared how she'd been lying on her back on a ridge watching a large raptor — she didn't know if it was a hawk or an eagle — soaring for nearly half-an-hour without flapping its wings. She said it got so high she had to use her binoculars to see it. Her insight was that, due to fear, she'd been resisting going in a certain direction in life even though there were many things pointing that way, including passion, abilities, and opportunities. She knew that if she simply "set her wings to catch the updraft" she would naturally go in that direction, and had, in fact, resolved to do so.

"That's a significant breakthrough, Jennifer," Len said. "As I'm sure you know, even with the 'updraft' there will be challenges and fresh fears to overcome. But the greatest fear most of us face is not the fear of our weakness and inability, but the fear of our true strength and potential. You've been released from that fear, and we want to affirm your new direction."

We all applauded her and Len added, "By the way, the bird you were watching was most certainly an eagle. If it didn't have a white head it was either an immature bald eagle or a golden eagle, though goldens are quite rare around here."

I shared next and told about my experiences on the "Live-With-in-Your-Limits" day. They all laughed when I described my reaction to the discovery that I couldn't cross the river. Then I shared how a significant part of my application was turning off the voices of people who were trying to impose their dreams on me. With some difficulty, I shared how I was going to have to confront a long-time, forceful friend, and how, if he wouldn't back off, I felt I needed to end the friendship.

Len responded, "The voices we allow to speak to us and in-fluence us — whether they are the voices of friends, books, or other media — these are the forces that shape us. You've made a powerful discovery that will give you increasing freedom for the rest of your life. Thanks for sharing."

Shane's lesson was from the "Processing Your Pain" stage. Like me, he'd been moved by the idea that pain will impact us, but need not define us. Specifically, his father had walked out when he was nine, and Shane realized on the trek that he'd been allowing that event to define him. He even used it as an excuse for his own marital and parenting shortcomings. He shared with us how on the day of his insight he'd literally cut a sapling, made a small stake, and hammered it into the trail. With deep emotion he said, "As I stepped past that stake and walked down the trail I yelled out, 'Dad, you hurt me a lot! But I will no longer allow your rejection to define me. I will be the husband and father you were not!'"

We were all moved. Len stood with wet eyes and simply said, "You've been released. You are not your father."

He then announced a debrief session at 7:30 in the conference room. Jennifer, Shane, and I visited in the dining room until then, telling story after story. In addition to her fall on the log, Jennifer had slid more than one hundred yards down a steep slope, bruising up her legs. Shane had incorrectly entered a set of coordinates and hadn't figured it out for several hours. He ended up finishing his day in the dark. We'd all seen deer and rabbits, squirrels and grouse. No one else had seen a fox or elk, but Shane was quite sure he'd seen a lynx. No cougars were spotted, but we wondered aloud how many had seen us.

At 7:30 we refilled our coffee mugs and went to the conference room. The entire staff was present, as on the opening night.

Len began his talk. "You've been on quite a journey. And if you're like others who have been here, the inner journey was even more challenging than the outer trails and trials. You each have an inherent capacity for growth and accomplishment, as amazing as nuclear energy. We hope you've learned that truth in a way you will never forget, and that you have also learned how to release and develop this capacity.

"Beyond the immediate benefit of the exercises you've been working through, our hope is that you will see the three phases as a template for future evaluation and planning.

Harnessing Your History is an ongoing process because you're always adding to your history. There will be new events that shape you in new ways, new experiences of pain and suffering, new encouragements, and the discovery of new gifts and abilities. As you age, there will be new limitations to live with. But always remember, those limits are gifts to help you focus your energy and efforts. Your history is the raw material that provides fuel for the release.

"*Focusing Your Future* is another process that calls for continued renewal. Carve out one or more full days, at least annually, to think through and adjust your destination, dreams, purpose, and goals. Keep firing those neutrons that initiate the chain reaction.

"*Mastering Your Moment* requires a more frequent introspection, at least weekly. This keeps the energy release from running amok. As you establish new goals you must develop new habits to support those goals. Whenever you notice a counterproductive pattern in your life, *Stop Spinning*! And always, always, always make sure there are partners in your life, cheerleaders, challengers, fellow adventurers on the journey.

"Tomorrow, we will have individual ninety-minute debriefs with each of you, two in the morning and one in the early afternoon. You are welcome to stay on site for two more nights if you want extra time to assimilate your learnings before you reenter your non-wilderness lives. You also have the option of a sixty-minute one-on-one meeting with me, during which I will share with you some of my journey and my understanding of how spirituality can play a significant role in our lives.

"In conclusion, never mistake the process we've given you for life itself. Never allow the reflective process to replace action. *Harness Your History, Focus Your Future*, but make sure you begin now to *Master Your Moment*. You do not live in the past. You do not live in the future. You live right now. One of my favorite sayings goes, 'Yesterday is history, tomorrow is a mystery, today is a gift, that's why they call it the present.' What are you doing with that present? Are you unwrapping it and making the most of it? Or are you squandering it?

"Take the gift of today, the meeting place of everything you are and everything you have experienced, everything you can be, everything you can do, and invest it in something you believe in, in the things that really matter to you. When you do, there will be a release of power and energy and creativity that will be for you, and for those you touch, as surprising and spectacular as the chain reaction that starts when one little neutron splits an atom and releases what was hidden, but always there. God bless you all as you continue your journeys."

As we applauded, I blinked back tears and saw Jennifer and Shane doing the same. I knew each of us had been changed — permanently.

We mingled for more than an hour, filling in the gaps in each of our stories. We also questioned Randy, Marsha, and Jonathon about their journeys. It turned out they'd always stayed in the camps just behind us, restocking supplies and doing any necessary clean up and repairs. By ten o'clock I was ready for bed. Sleep came easily.

Day 14, and Beyond

No one called me for breakfast, and by the time I got mobile, the others were just about finished. They laughed at my bleary eyes and constant yawning.

Shane was in a hurry to get home to his family, so he took the 8:30 debrief. Jennifer took the 10:30. I was content with the afternoon session since I planned to stay for another night. We said goodbye to Shane after exchanging email addresses. Jennifer left right after lunch.

My debrief session was an expansion of what Len had said the night before. We walked through my personal reflections from the trek — as much as I was willing to share. Len asked questions and offered insights to help round out my thinking. He had some friends who worked in the area of child poverty, and promised to send me their contact info and let them know I might be calling. At the end of the ninety minutes, Len asked if I wanted the optional one-hour spirituality session.

"Absolutely," I said. "That's one of the reasons I'm staying for another night." We agreed to meet that evening at seven.

*****

The one-hour evening session stretched into two. While the ten days on my own had been revolutionary, and the personal debrief gave me more tools to continue with the new directions I'd set, the session on spirituality opened up an entirely new chapter in my life. Len explained in very specific detail how I could connect with the Creator in a personal, even intimate way. He helped me understand how I could integrate spirituality into the full spectrum of my life, rather than isolating it in a separate compartment. He didn't answer all my questions, but suggested avenues for further exploration. In short, as my outdoor adventure ended, a new phase of my spiritual journey began. And it continues to this day, adding energy, creativity, direction, and passion to every facet of my life.

For related "Adventure of the Soul" resources,
or information on booking the author to speak,
please visit

www.adventureofthesoul.com